# THE DREAM SEASON

NORTHWESTERN'S MIRACULOUS
MARCH TO THE 1996 ROSE BOWL

Chicago Sun-Times Features, Inc.
401 N. Wabash Ave.
Chicago, Illinois 60611

ISBN  Hardback: 1-888682-00-0
ISBN  Paperback: 1-888682-01-9

# THE DREAM SEASON

## NORTHWESTERN'S MIRACULOUS MARCH TO THE 1996 ROSE BOWL

BY THE SPORTS STAFF OF THE CHICAGO SUN-TIMES

INTRODUCTION BY RICK TELANDER

PUBLISHED BY

## Performance Media
CHICAGO SUN-TIMES FEATURES, INC.

# TEAM ZENITH SALUTES TEAM NORTHWESTERN

## Congratulations on a picture perfect season.

 *The Quality Goes In Before The Name Goes On.*

N9582-12

# CONTENTS

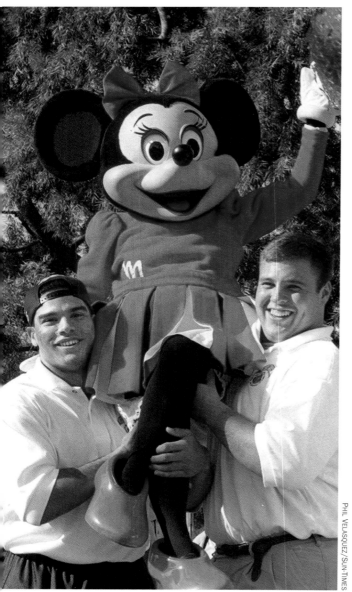

PHIL VELASQUEZ/SUN-TIMES

**Even the NU players found themselves believing in fairy tales.**

*This year's team somehow has found the cure for intellectually-induced passivity.*

# THIS WAS NO FABLE... '95 CATS ARE A LEGEND

*BY RICK TELANDER*

Fabulist creatures that we are, we need a big metaphor to help us understand the 1995 Northwestern football team.

And so we have come up with—ta da!—*Cinderella.*

Almost every story about these feisty Wildcat overachievers has used the *Cinderella* comparison at some point in its analysis. Famous Los Angeles Times sports columnist Jim Murray spent so much time making NU-*Cinderella* comparisons in his post-Rose Bowl story, no one was sure when he'd slip out of fairyland and come back to reality.

Me, I probably used the *Cinderella* motif once or twice in my own Northwestern coverage this past year. But not a lot. That's because I'm not so sure it's the best fable that applies to these nationally-ranked, Big Ten champions.

Consider that *Cinderella* was always pretty, always a winner; it just took some nice clothes, a new hairstyle, and a lost slipper to get people to notice. Not so with Northwestern. The school itself long has been fine, but its football teams could have been dressed in tuxedos and Superman capes and still never beaten Notre Dame, Michigan and Penn State, as they did this season.

Moreover, I tend to get *Cinderella* confused with all the other mythic gals of yore—*Sleeping Beauty, Goldilocks, Rapunzel, Snow White,* the *Princess and the Pea. Snow White* and her seven dwarfs might have worked as a parallel for previous Wildcat teams, I suppose, if you were referring to the NU quarterback and the defensive front.

But the heroine in each of those fables needed some kind of divine     assistance to achieve her goals.

Not these Cats. Their divine assistance was all their own. Coach Gary Barnett channeled the players' energy and desire and funneled it to a fine victorious point, but there was no magic wand or sorcerer or handsome prince appearing suddenly to save the day. This was a team thing, done from within.

Perhaps a more fitting tale to represent this Northwestern team is *The Crow and the Pitcher*. Remember that one? A thirsty crow sees water at the bottom of a pitcher, but cannot reach it. Rather than despair, the crow tirelessly drops pebble after pebble into the container until finally the water has reached the brim and he can drink. Right there, you have the Northwestern boys performing their ritual, tirelessly practicing through the winter, spring, and summer, so that in the fall, their logical, one-pebble-at-a-time approach allows them to do what no one thought they could do: drink from the winner's cup.

*You must remember that what Northwestern did this past season couldn't be done.*

**Darnell Autry helped write a fable that began over 47 years ago, by leading his teammates to Northwestern's second Rose Bowl.**

# INTRODUCTION

*Coach Gary Barnett channeled the players' energy and desire and funneled it to a fine victorious point.*

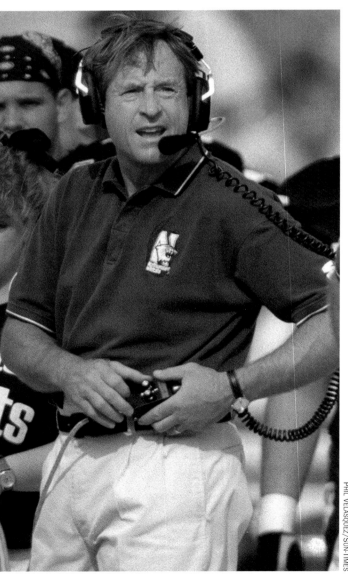

**Coach Gary Barnett channeled the energy of the team to make this a dream season.**

You must remember that what Northwestern did this past season couldn't be done. It simply couldn't. Until now, the last winning NU team was the 1971 squad that went 7-4 and was preceded by the 1970 team which finished 6-4. Neither of those teams won the Big Ten or went to a bowl game; indeed, at almost any other Big Ten school such records would have been considered, at best, nice and, at worst, grounds for firing the coach. At NU they took on the glow of sanctity. That is because before and after those two teams lay a combined 31-year wasteland of football ineptitude, spanning six coaches, hundreds of players and thousands of bad Northwestern-is-a-wimp jokes.

Consider this past season the Wildcats won as many games, 10, as the team won from 1976 to 1984. The culture of gridiron failure was so well established at Northwestern that a coach could go from 2-8-1 one season to 0-11 the next, as Francis Peay did from 1988 to 1989, and still not lose his job.

The problem with turning things around at the school was, of course, the academic standards and, in a kind of Catch-22 injustice, the losing tradition itself. Hacking through that tradition must have been like swimming out of a tar pit for Barnett and his boys. Getting smart players to play like cavemen must have been equally tough. But they did it.

A club that from 1976 to 1981 had produced a record of 3-62-1 abruptly found itself going undefeated in eight Big Ten games. The 69 points the 1995 Wildcat defense gave up in those conference games was 13 less than Michigan State alone scored on NU in 1989.

Back in the old losing days it was never clear that Northwestern should even *be* in the Big Ten, let alone have a chance to win the thing. There were valiant but doomed players then, such as cornerback Roosevelt Groves, who started from 1979 to 1982, and who mostly hung on for dear life while afield. Groves still holds the team career touchdown-save record, 15, and in my montage memory, I recall him as a skinny defensive back endlessly being dragged closer to the goal line by faceless wide receivers and tailbacks. Groves had a double major—nuclear engineering and mechanical engineering—and he once noted that his academic and athletic aspirations didn't "really fit together" unless you figured that "splitting a receiver from the ball is like splitting an atom."

JON SALL/SUN-TIMES

Evanston Mayor Lorraine H. Morton wanted to make the 1995 season a permanent memory by commemorating the Big Ten championship at the entrance to the city.

This year's team somehow has found the cure for intellectually-induced passivity. These kids are smart—the team's SAT scores are second nationally only to Stanford's—and yet tough as iron rods. Their half-time adjustments enabled them to play better in the third and fourth quarters than any NU team in memory. "You could only make the half-time changes we do with smart kids," acknowledged defensive backs coach Jerry Brown, himself a former Wildcat player.

This team caught the attention of the nation, because of its heart, its manners and its shedding of the same type of you-can't-do-that mantle so many of us seem to carry through life.

"We came from nowhere," is how Barnett puts it. And when you get right down to it, didn't we all?

The Notre Dame game started everything. The Wildcats had been brought in to South Bend in the season opener to be the Domers' first victim en route to a national championship season. Trouble was, the sacrificial goat

*Back in the old losing days it was never clear that Northwestern should even **be** in the Big Ten, let alone have a chance to win the thing.*

wouldn't die. Not only that, it turned on its host and started biting and kicking for all it was worth.

I was at that game, and I barely breathed during the second half. I guarantee you, I didn't move. The Wildcats won, 17-15, and if there ever has been a larger group of silent people gathered in one spot, well, it could only have been at Michigan Stadium, four weeks later, when the Cats shocked the Wolverines, 19-13.

*Suddenly, Purple Passion gripped folks everywhere.*

Suddenly, Purple Passion gripped folks everywhere. *Why, if those kids can do that, maybe there is justice in the world!*

I recalled the time my Northwestern teammates and I were playing Southern California way back in 1969. It was a hot night at the Los Angeles Coliseum and each time USC scored, which was constantly, a man dressed as a Trojan warrior would gallop around the stadium in celebration on his great white horse Traveler II. After the fifth or sixth USC touchdown, the horse collapsed in the end zone. My pal, NU running back Mike Adamle, who would win the Big Ten MVP award in 1970, turned to me on the bench and said in shock, "My God, we killed Traveler II."

Cheerleaders and fans alike were part of the miracle of taking the Purple to Pasadena.

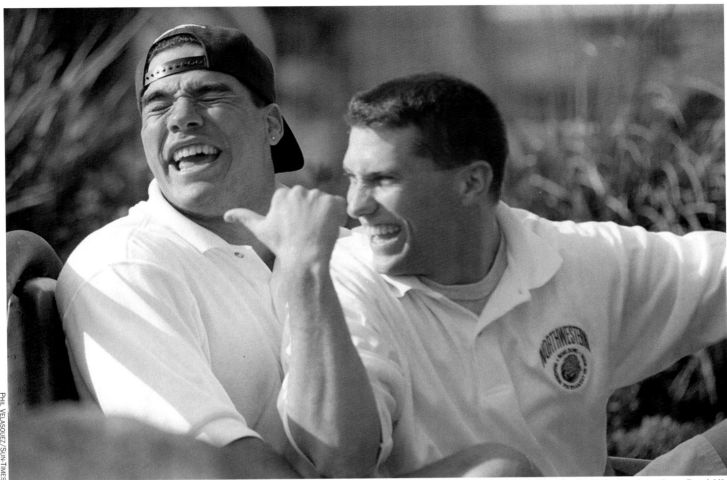

PHIL VELASQUEZ/SUN-TIMES

It's been a heck of a ride for the **NU** Wildcats this year, proving they were on the right track just like the "Little Engine that Could."

Those days are gone, thank you. The only thing the new NU football team kills these days are the naysayers.

And thus, the most appropriate fable comes firmly to mind. It's the story called *The Little Engine Who Could.*

The mountain is there, but the little train that has no business making it to the peak and beyond just keeps chugging away. "*I think I can. I think I can,*" the little engine says. It's corny, you bet, but so is every fairy tale.

So come aboard, folks. Grab a seat behind Coach Barnett who's riding up there in the little cab with all his assistants. Pat Fitzgerald and Darnell Autry and Steve Schnur will make room for you. Chant along with Sam Valenzisi and D'Wayne Bates and Matt Rice and Chris Martin and Rob Johnson and William Bennett and all the other Wildcats who are hanging out the windows, singing their song.

*I think I can. I think I can.*

It's one heck of a ride.

**The most appropriate fable comes firmly to mind. It's the story called "The Little Engine Who Could."**

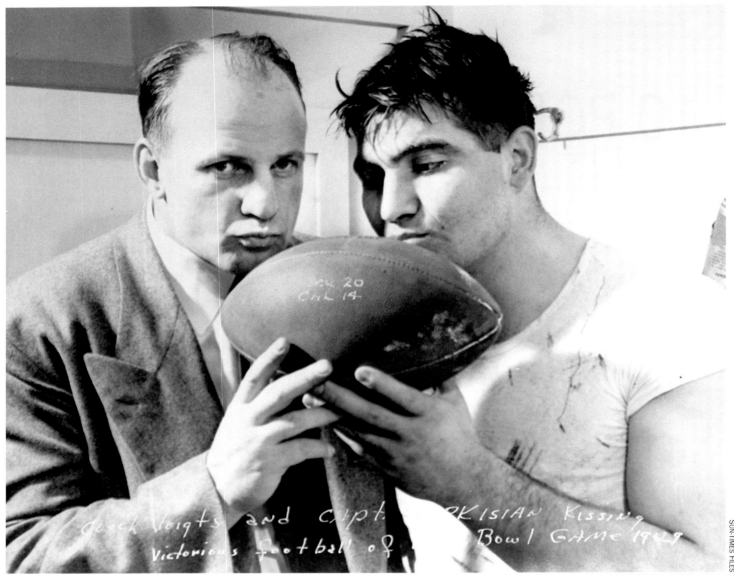

**Coach Bob Voigts and his team captain, Alex Sarkisian, kiss the victorious football of the Rose Bowl Game of 1949 in which NU beat California 20-14.**

*From 1949 until this fall, Northwestern had only nine winning seasons. The Wildcats' record during that span was 133-326-8.*

season's miracles. It elevated the Wildcats, who still were being coached by Parseghian, to No. 1 in the nation.

The largest crowd in Dyche Stadium history (55,752) showed up to watch a quarterback duel between NU's Tom Myers and Notre Dame's Daryle Lamonica. It was no contest. Myers completed 11 of 18 passes for 168 yards and threw touchdown tosses of 23 and seven yards to Paul Flatley. The Wildcats won at Indiana the next week before injuries led to their fall from No. 1.

**Sept. 23, 1967:** NU 12, Miami (Fla.) 7: Miami, which was led by defensive star Ted Hendricks, was ranked No. 1 for the season opener at Dyche. The Wildcats pulled off the upset before 38,780 on halfback Chico Kurzawski's nine-yard scoring pass to quarterback Bill Melzer for the game-winning touchdown.

Melzer, who also scored the first NU touchdown, passed for 91 yards and rushed for another 43. Kurzawski made a big contribution with quick kicks, which became his trademark at NU. He boomed one for 65 yards and another for 68. NU lost their next four games and finished 3-7 under Alex Agase.

**Nov. 13, 1971:** NU 14, Ohio State 10: Agase was still in charge when the Wildcats won for the last time in Columbus, Ohio.

Greg Strunk shocked a crowd of 86,062 with a 93-yard kickoff return in the first quarter, and Randy Anderson plowed a yard for the game-winning touchdown in the

*The largest crowd in Dyche Stadium history (55,752) showed up to watch a quarterback duel between NU's Tom Myers and Notre Dame's Daryle Lamonica. It was no contest.*

PHIL VELASQUEZ/SUN-TIMES

Alex Sarkisian, the captain of the Wildcats' 1948 team, remembers his winning trip to the Rose Bowl in 1949.

**Like this season's squad, the 1948 Wildcats under Coach Bob Voigts played some big regular-season games before being extended their Rose Bowl invitation.**

fourth. The Wildcats beat Michigan State the next week to finish 7-4, their last winning season until 1995.

**Sept. 25, 1982:** NU 31, Northern Illinois 7: This one was big for a different reason: It brought an end to the nation's longest losing streak at 34 games.

Ricky Edwards rushed for 177 yards and a school record-tying four touchdowns and Sandy Schwab passed for 212 yards. One of Edwards' scores came on an 80-yard run, but only 22,078 attended at Dyche. Afterward, students tore down the goalposts and drowned them in Lake Michigan. That started a tradition that didn't please the NU administration.

The Wildcats were pounded 45-7 by Iowa the next week and finished 3-8, good enough to make Dennis Green the Big Ten coach of the year.

**Oct. 26, 1991:** NU 17, Illinois 11: No Northwestern victory in the last 45 years was greeted with as much emotion as this one on the field. Rodney Ray, now a fifth-year cornerback for the Wildcats, rushed for the first NU touchdown and Len Williams, who completed 10 of 19 passes for 141 yards, scored the eventual game-winner on a four-yard plunge in the third quarter.

**Nov. 2, 1991:** NU 16, Michigan State 13: Coach Francis Peay appeared to have the NU program turned around after this victory, the Wildcats' first in a Big Ten road game in five years. The game-winner came on a seven-yard touchdown pass from Len Williams to Mark Benson with 1:48 to play on a frigid day in East Lansing, Mich. Benson had 10 receptions, Ed Sutter 12 unassisted tackles and Williams 201 passing yards. But the Wildcats lost their final three games, and Peay's contract was not renewed after the season.

**Oct. 3, 1992:** NU 28, Purdue 14: Maybe this one doesn't seem big now, but it triggered what is happening in Evanston this season. Gary Barnett's first victory after three nonconference losses was NU's first in West Lafayette, Ind., in 42 years.

**Sept. 2, 1995:** NU 17, Notre Dame 15: Who would have believed this one? D'Wayne Bates, who was playing in his first college game, made his first reception and the game-winning touchdown in South Bend, Ind.

The Wildcats were 24-point underdogs, and no NU victory was greeted with as much national attention—not even the Rose Bowl triumph. For two weeks, there was giddiness in Evanston. Then Miami of Ohio paid the Wildcats a visit.

**Oct. 7, 1995:** NU 19, Michigan 13: NU's first victory in Ann Arbor since 1959 stamped the Wildcats, who entered the game as 16-point underdogs, as Big Ten title contenders.

The key came early, when NU linebacker Pat Fitzgerald stopped Wolverines tailback Tim Biakabutuka twice for losses to ignite a goal-line stand at the start of the second quarter before 104,642. Four Sam Valenzisi field goals were the bulk of the offense, and NU hasn't slowed down since.

*Northwestern University opened the 1948 campaign with a 19-0 triumph at UCLA and a 21-0 victory against Purdue at Dyche Stadium. Even though Michigan finished as the national champion in 1948, and Notre Dame wound up second, Northwestern finished seventh after beating California 20-14 in the Rose Bowl.*

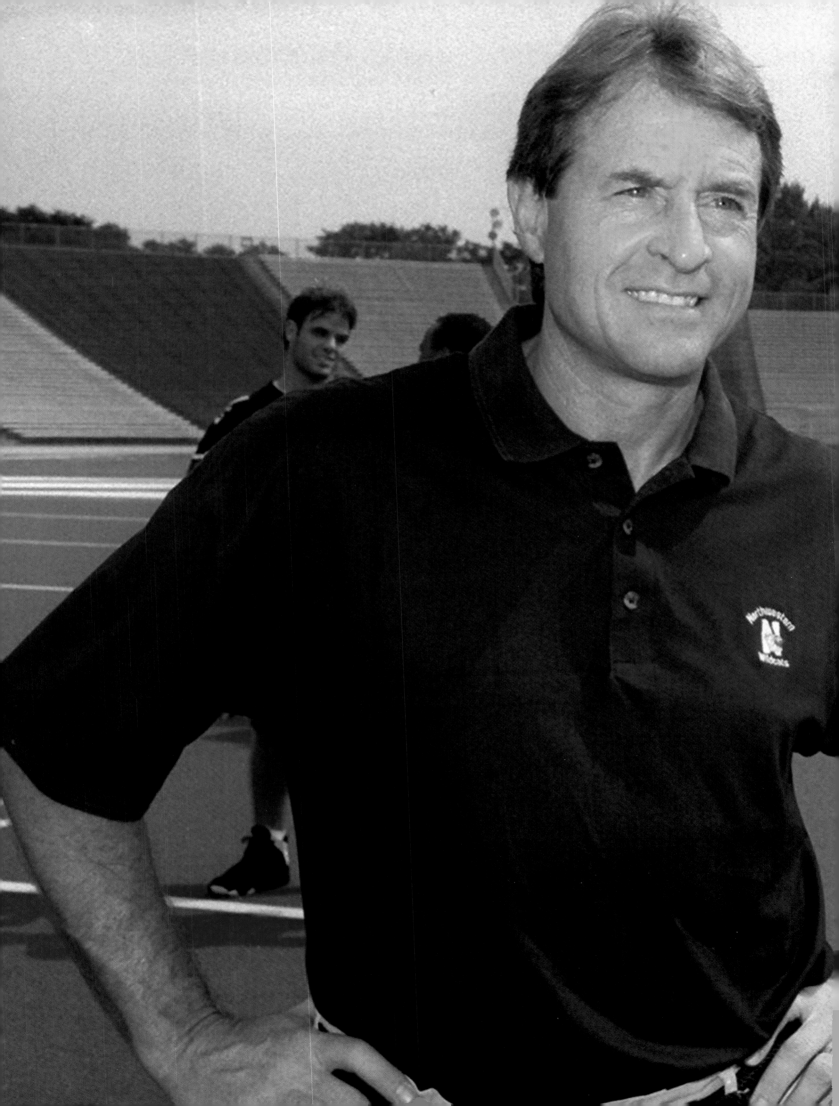

# COACH OF THE YEAR

## BARNETT BUILDS FOOTBALL POWER

*BY DAN BICKLEY*

It's clear one of the longest-running jokes in college football is officially over.

Northwestern University—once the very symbol of futility—is a big winner this season, with high rankings in team and coaches' polls.

Coach Gary Barnett is the architect of the improbable, and following road victories against such favorites as Notre Dame and Michigan, he is the leader in what could be one of the best coaching jobs in history.

It appears he is doing what no one could accomplish in the past 35 years: Build Northwestern into a football power.

"People don't think you can change things," said Barnett, who was named the 1995 winner of the Bear Bryant Award as the college football coach of the year.

"People just don't believe you can go about things the right way and get things changed. No one wants change, no one accepts change, so it's hard for them to believe it. But if you look over history, it happens all the time."

But at Northwestern, where the chemistry lab is deemed as important as the football team? Have the stringent academic requirements loosened just a bit?

"The answer is no, absolutely not," Northwestern president Henry S. Bienen said. "In all respects, he understands the values of Northwestern, and he's never interested in bending those values. He wants to have a strong football program within those parameters."

*"One of the biggest things he preaches is the power of the human mind."*
*— NU's Steve Schnur*

PHIL VELASQUEZ/SUN-TIMES

**Coach Gary Barnett gave Northwestern a rock solid plan to win the 1995 season.**

But how is Barnett succeeding where everyone from Rick Venturi to Dennis Green to Francis Peay failed?

"I can't answer that," Bienen said. "But I'm not going to look a gift horse in the mouth."

Indeed, Bienen is so happy he has agreed to spend $20 million to further level the playing field. Of that money, $17 million will go toward renovation for Dyche Stadium, $3 million to construction of an indoor athletic facility.

So, who is the man behind the curtain, the one pushing all the right buttons and concocting this fairy tale in just his fourth year at the helm?

"He is the most determined guy I've ever known," Wildcats quarterback Steve Schnur said.

Indeed, when Barnett recruited Schnur—a star quarterback from St. Louis—the coach's lofty goals almost seemed absurd given his school's enigmatic past.

"It's hard to talk to coach Barnett about Northwestern football without coming away thinking one of two things," Schnur said. "Either the guy is completely crazy, or he's pretty darned determined. I chose No. 2, and that's why I'm here."

Make no mistake, Barnett's plan is rock solid. It starts with an emphasis on nationwide recruiting, thereby finding enough talented players to fit within Northwestern's admission requirements.

"We've been very aggressive," Barnett said. "Our line has been that whoever comes in here and turns this thing around will be the guys who are forever remembered in our program. If you go into an established program, you're just another guy.

"And every kid who can get into this school knows they should come here. But they can't pull the trigger because they want the experience that a Michigan can give them…they want the thrills, the highs, the bowl games, the watches, the mementos you eventually throw away. So they have to trust that they can win here."

Now they can. The mindset finally has been changed.

"One of the biggest things he preaches is the power of the human mind," Schnur said. "He gave us the story this year of how, under hypnosis, they can tell you a tape recorder weighs 300 pounds. When you wake up, they tell you to pick up the tape recorder, and you can't. So when you start buying into things like that…"

Down go Notre Dame and Michigan.

"Right," Schnur said. "Maybe on paper Michigan is better than us. But when you believe, it can be a powerful thing."

Practicing for the big time, Barnett, 49, never believed he would become one of the hottest commodities in coaching.

A star quarterback in high school, he played under Dan Devine at Missouri. He spent two years as a graduate assistant at Missouri and two years as offensive coordinator at Air Academy High School in Colorado Springs, Colo.

He became head coach at Air Academy in 1973, compiling a 69-23 record in nine years. Not exactly on the fast track.

"I've always been real happy to be where I was at the time," he said. "I never thought about the next step."

For Barnett, that came in 1982, when he was about to make a lateral move and coach Rampart High School in Colorado Springs. But the job at Fort Lewis College in Durango, Colo. opened up, and Barnett was the man.

Fort Lewis, a Division II school, went 4-5-1 and 4-6 in Barnett's two seasons. But he changed the team's attitude—and after he left, the Skyhawks won their conference championship.

"With the players that Gary recruited," said Jim Etzler, a defensive lineman who played for Barnett at Fort Lewis, "he took a mediocre football program and turned it around. He was able to take players who weren't exactly super athletes, and make them play like they were. He left, and the other coaches who came in rode the foundation he had built."

Perhaps the most influential day in Barnett's life came when he was hired in 1984 as running backs coach for Colorado University. He worked under Bill McCartney for eight years and witnessed the rise of a dormant program. In 1984, Colorado finished 1-10. Six years later, the Buffaloes won a national championship. McCartney since has left Colorado, but his impact on Barnett is undeniable.

"I think Gary saw a side of college athletics from (McCartney) that he had never seen before," said Louisiana State coach Gerry DiNardo, an assistant with Barnett at Colorado. "Things like there are certain ways to act during a pregame meal, ways to act on a road trip, that there is something to hard work, that there are more important things than talent, that a team like Northwestern can go to the Rose Bowl."

PHIL VELASQUEZ/SUN-TIMES

"One of the biggest things he preaches is the power of the human mind," said NU quaterback Steve Schnur.

# A SEASON TO REMEMBER

## PERFECT ENDING TO MAGICAL YEAR

*BY JAY MARIOTTI*

Three…two…one…and not a soul woke up. It happened. The one thing that never could happen in sports happened. The snowball survived in hell, the cow jumped over the moon and Northwestern went an entire Big Ten football season without losing a conference game.

One last time, you thumped the forehead, blinked again and again. But the famous final scene did not disappear, nor will it ever, headed instead to the archives that preserve the most special of life's lessons: Absolutely anything is possible. You didn't have to be an NU grad to stand on this field in the middle of nowhere and begin to smile, feel a tear ready to trickle.

From one sideline raced the NU players, hugging and hollering and raising their helmets to the sky. From the other side came the NU fans, running aimlessly, chanting "Big Ten Champs!" and other unthinkables. They created an exuberant purple mosh pit, isolated from the world in the heartland darkness, partying to the point that the p.a. man had to announce, "We congratulate the Wildcats for a great season, but please leave the field so the marching band can perform."

And at that moment, for the first time, the big, lovable absurdity of it all began to sink in. Oh my God, they did it. They didn't blow it, as their predecessors annually insisted. They did it.

"We're a big-time program," Coach Gary Barnett declared after his 1995 miracle regular season was done,

# THE 1995 DREAM SEASON

### SEPTEMBER 2
**NORTHWESTERN 17, NOTRE DAME 15**
*This season opener was coined the "The Upset of the Century" because NU had not beaten the Irish since 1962. The Wildcats never trailed after Dave Beazley caught a seven-yard touchdown pass from Steve Schnur with 8:45 left in the first quarter. Sam Valenzisi set the NU record for consecutive extra points and kicked a 35-yard field goal, Darnell Autry rushed for 160 yards on 33 carries and D'Wayne Bates' first collegiate reception went for a 26-yard touchdown that provided the decisive points in the third quarter.*

### SEPTEMBER 16
**MIAMI OF OHIO 30, NORTHWESTERN 28**
*The euphoria built from the Notre Dame upset lasted one week. NU, a 16-point favorite in the Dyche Stadium opener, blew a 28-7 fourth-quarter lead. Miami backup quarterback Sam Ricketts misfired on a two-point conversion pass that would have given the Redskins the lead with 2:22 remaining, but even that gift couldn't save the Wildcats.*

### SEPTEMBER 23
**NORTHWESTERN 30, AIR FORCE 6**
*Air Force became NU's first Dyche Stadium victim in 12 games, the Wildcats having gone 0-10-1 since beating Wake Forest in the third game of the 1993 season. Linebacker Pat Fitzgerald had 11 tackles, a sack, an interception and a fumble recovery against a team ranked third in the nation in rushing coming in. The Wildcats kept the Falcons out of the end zone.*

### SEPTEMBER 30
**NORTHWESTERN 31, INDIANA 7**
*The Wildcats reached 3-1 for the first time since 1963 and beat the Hoosiers at Dyche Stadium for the first time since 1984. Indiana lost star tailback Alex Smith to a serious rib injury in the teams' Big Ten opener. Darnell Autry had another big day, gaining 162 yards on 28 carries and scoring two touchdowns. The game swung on Brian Musso's 86-yard punt return with NU nursing a 13-7 third-quarter lead.*

### OCTOBER 7
**NORTHWESTERN 19, MICHIGAN 13**
*The Wildcats beat Michigan for the first time since 1965 and won in Ann Arbor for the first time since 1959 in front of a disbelieving 104,642. Darnell Autry kept his 100-yard streak alive, thanks to a 28-yard run on his last carry. Four field goals by Sam Valenzisi and a tricky 26-yard pass from D'Wayne Bates to tight end Darren Drexler, which set up Steve Schnur's two-yard TD pass to sophomore fullback Matt Hartl, provided the necessary offense.*

### OCTOBER 14
**NORTHWESTERN 27, MINNESOTA 17**
*The Wildcats found a new way to win, rallying from a 14-3 deficit on three Darnell Autry touchdowns in the Metrodome. It was the Wildcats' fourth consecutive win at an opponent's homecoming. This one was not pretty. Sam Valenzisi's extra-point streak ended at 48 when his last kick hit the upright. Paul Burton had one punt blocked and another went three yards. Autry lost his first fumble of the season.*

**Northwestern Wildcats celebrate a spectacular season after their final win,**

accented with a methodical 23-8 victory over Purdue. "I couldn't have given you a date, but honest, I knew we were going to win a Big Ten title. Hopefully, what we've started here is a pattern and a legacy."

He couldn't wait to get back to Evanston, where he would walk over to a chart in the football building. On it was something he wrote four years ago, when he took the job no one wanted. It said: Big Ten title, 199? "I'm gonna go paint that in," he said, finally allowing himself a grin, a little relief after weeks of blinding attention and stress.

Can you believe it? Northwestern put up double-digit wins for the first time ever. They won a share of the conference title for the first time since 1936. Their defense, even without leader Pat Fitzgerald, completed a dominating year in which it allowed only 21 second-half points over the last nine games. Their Hollywood running back, Darnell Autry, was a legit Heisman

securing their Big Ten Championship title.

JON SALL/SUN-TIMES

# THE 1995 DREAM SEASON

**OCTOBER 21**
NORTHWESTERN 35, WISCONSIN 0
*Coach Gary Barnett won his first homecoming game as, finally, the crowd turned out. The 49,256 spectators represented the first sellout of Dyche Stadium since 1983. Wisconsin made seven turnovers, so winning the game wasn't difficult. It was the Wildcats' first shutout victory against a Big Ten opponent since a 30-0 blitz of Indiana in 1975 and Wisconsin's worst defeat since 1943.*

**OCTOBER 28**
NORTHWESTERN 17, ILLINOIS 14
*NU, now ranked No. 8 in the country, spoiled another homecoming after coming back from a 14-3 deficit. Brian Gowins, Sam Valenzisi's backup, provided the winning points with a 49-yard field goal, but the outcome wasn't clinched until Eric Collier's second interception of the game came in the end zone with seven seconds remaining. D'Wayne Bates' 34-yard touchdown reception from Steve Schnur and Darnell Autry's 151 yards on a career-high 41 carries provided just enough offense.*

**NOVEMBER 4**
NORTHWESTERN 21, PENN STATE 10
*The Wildcats were underdogs for the fifth time and foiled the oddsmakers again. In what might have been their most inspired performance of the season, they scored on their first possession with a 73-yard drive and rode the defense the rest of the way. The Wildcats snapped Penn State's 10-game road winning streak and 20-game streak on artificial turf.*

**NOVEMBER 11**
NORTHWESTERN 31, IOWA 20
*A week-long war of words between NU players and Iowa coach Hayden Fry set the stage for the Wildcats to snap a 21-game losing streak against the Hawkeyes. Again they fell behind 14-3, but Darnell Autry's 10th consecutive game of 100-plus rushing yards brought them back, even after Pat Fitzgerald broke his leg in the third quarter. The game was still in doubt until Rodney Ray forced a fumble and Hudhaifa Ismaeli returned the ball 31 yards for a touchdown with 2:56 to play.*

**NOVEMBER 18**
NORTHWESTERN 23, PURDUE 8
*The Wildcats continued their businesslike ways to clinch a share of their first Big Ten title since 1936. Chris Martin's 76-yard interception return got them on the board, and a 72-yard pass from Steve Schnur to D'Wayne Bates made it 14-0 at halftime. Chris Martin's blocked punt for a safety and Darnell Autry's 59-yard run to the one early in the third quarter gave the Cats a 23-0 lead, and they coasted in, with a winning season.*

candidate. The man who put it together, Barnett, not only won Coach of the Year, but deserves being a candidate for Coach of the Century.

The zeroes always were on the other side of the ledger, such as the 0-8 conference record two years ago, or the 0-11 season in 1989, or the 0-11 year in 1981. But in 1995, the record reads 8-0, and it is not written in erasable ink. If only they hadn't lost to Miami of Ohio, the big-picture record also would be without blemish.

"It's so crazy, it's hard to realize it's happening," said Steve Schnur, the rock-steady quarterback. "I'd be lying if I said I expected this. It's hard to put into words."

"We believed all along. And now, everyone believes," Autry said. "It was incredible out there, people telling me, 'Thank you. It's been so long.' What a feeling. I'll never forget it."

Nor will we.

29

# THE 'CATS ARE BACK...33 YEARS LATER

## IRISH'S FIRST LOSS SINCE 1962

*BY RICK TELANDER*

Ohmygod.

If anybody blinks, do they change the score?

Northwestern 17, Notre Dame 15.

Sweet, suffering Touchdown Jesus.

We're not talking halftime score.

Not first downs.

Not the average of each team's IQ divided by eight.

Bless us, father, for Notre Dame has sinned. It has been 33 years since its last confession—excuse us, loss—to NU. 17-15, my friends, is what is known in college football circles as a final score.

In fact, it's so final, it's over and out.

Notre Dame must carry this defeat into the cold dark night like an icy mortal sin because these two teams, after decades of competition and thousands—well, dozens of Notre Dame victories—are not scheduled to play each other again in this century.

They're not scheduled to play again, period.

"We'll catch 'em in a bowl game, maybe," said Northwestern coach Gary Barnett after the game.

Heresy?

The truth is Notre Dame has now lost five of its last 8 games, and even though the Irish opened the season ranked No. 9 in the nation, at this point perennial patsy NU has the inside track on a bowl game that might not even want the underachievers from Notre Dame.

This was not a fluke.

RICHARD A. CHAPMAN/SUN-TIMES

## TOP 25

| | TEAM | RECORD |
|---|---|---|
| 1. | FLORIDA ST. | (1-0) |
| 2. | NEBRASKA | (1-0) |
| 3. | TEXAS A&M | (1-0) |
| 4. | PENN ST. | (0-0) |
| 5. | FLORIDA | (1-0) |
| 6. | AUBURN | (1-0) |
| 7. | SOUTHERN CAL | (0-0) |
| 8. | TENNESSEE | (1-0) |
| 9. | OHIO ST. | (1-0) |
| 10. | COLORADO | (1-0) |
| 11. | MICHIGAN | (2-0) |
| 12. | UCLA | (1-0) |
| 13. | ALABAMA | (1-0) |
| 14. | OKLAHOMA | (0-0) |
| 15. | TEXAS | (1-0) |
| 16. | VIRGINIA | (1-1) |
| 17. | ARIZONA | (1-0) |
| 18. | WASHINGTON | (1-0) |
| 19. | MIAMI | (0-1) |
| 20. | VIRGINIA TECH | (0-0) |
| 21. | KANSAS ST. | (1-0) |
| 22. | SYRACUSE | (1-0) |
| 23. | N. CAROLINA ST. | (1-0) |
| 24. | OREGON | (1-0) |
| 25. | NOTRE DAME | (0-1) |

*This was not a fluke. Northwestern tailback Darnell Autry carried the ball 33 times for 160 net yards. NU quarterback Steve Schnur completed 14 of 28 passes for 166 yards and two touchdowns.*

Northwestern tailback Darnell Autry carried the ball 33 times for 160 net yards. NU quarterback Steve Schnur completed 14 of 28 passes for 166 yards and two touchdowns.

Notre Dame looked like a team without a clue.

Whenever it seemed Knute or Ara or Rudy or even Rick Mirer might offer some divine intervention on Notre Dame's poor offensive behalf, the spirit of Gerry Faust would lurch forward instead.

Kicker Kevin Kopka inexplicably missed his first extra point of the game.

Quarterback Ron Powlus simply tripped and fell down on his two-point attempt that could have tied the game late in the fourth quarter.

Tailback Randy Kinder was stopped from his power I-back position on fourth and two at Notre Dame's 45 with four minutes to go and the Irish set to drive down and kick a field goal for your basic 18-17, last-second win.

But Northwestern had more to do with this remarkable fold-up than a lot of Irish boosters might want to admit.

"They beat us fair and square," said Notre Dame's leading rusher Robert Farmer (85 yards on 16 carries). "No magic."

Nope, but there was some fire and smoke.

Kinder was stopped on that last plunge by an NU defensive wave that featured undersized defensive tackle Matt Rice at the gnarly crest.

"I wasn't thinking much," said Rice of the play. "I felt like I could bench 6,000 pounds. I was just blowing through there, taking whatever was around. The whole defense was playing with its hair on fire."

Barnett may have been on fire as a coach, but outwardly he stayed as calm as a glass of ice-water. He told his players not to carry him off the field, to act like they'd been in this spot before. In fact, he ordered them not to carry him off.

And he did this before the game.

"This is something we have visualized for four years," he said.

His players weren't nervous, he added, because "they have no idea of the significance of this game."

OK, youngsters, let's put this in perspective for you. This was Northwestern's biggest win since, since Illinois in 1991?

RICHARD A. CHAPMAN/SUN-TIMES

**Turnovers by Notre Dame were a deciding factor in Northwestern's stunning upset. Here, NU's Danny Sutter recovered.**

Ohio State in 1971?

California in the 1949 Rose Bowl?

Nah, Illinois wasn't that great a team in '91; NU was pretty darn good in 1971; the Rose Bowl team finished 8-2.

OK, young Cats, this was Northwestern's biggest upset win in the history of the whole eggheaded school.

Can you download that, fellows?

Calm and methodical, this is also a spirited squad.

Star runner Autry got a gut-wrenching unsportsmanlike conduct penalty called on him when he threw up his arms in celebration after his crucial fourth quarter 26-yard scamper to Notre Dame's four.

"I got in trouble because I did the rah-rah, sis-boom-bah in front of our fans," he said sheepishly.

And Notre Dame's reward?

A losing streak that may last forever.

*"I wasn't thinking much, I felt like I could bench 6,000 pounds. I was just blowing through there, taking whatever was around. The whole defense was playing with its hair on fire."*

*—NU's Matt Rice*

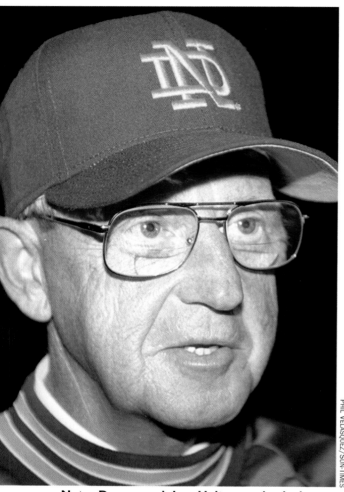

PHIL VELASQUEZ/SUN-TIMES

**Notre Dame coach Lou Holtz was shocked by the loss.**

*This one probably was NU's biggest football moment since the 1949 Rose Bowl victory against California.*

# THE UPSET OF THE CENTURY

## BELIEVE IT: NU STUNS NOTRE DAME

*BY LEN ZIEHM*

Gary Barnett has had some encouraging victories since taking over a downtrodden Northwestern football program.

There were the upsets of Illinois and Wisconsin in 1991, Barnett's first in Evanston, and the 1992 stunner against Boston College. The 1994 victory at Indiana was big, too, but all those triumphs are miniscule compared to this 17-15 shocker against Notre Dame.

This one probably was NU's biggest football moment since the 1949 Rose Bowl victory against California. It greatly impressed the 59,075 who packed Notre Dame Stadium, though the NU players were hardly awestruck.

"History is history," linebacker Pat Fitzgerald said. "You read about it in books. We can only take care of the future."

Barnett was confident that would be done in the last game of a four-year series between the nearby rivals, even though the Irish had hammered the Wildcats 14 consecutive times since NU's last win in 1962.

"Before we left the hotel I told my players I didn't want to be carried off the field," Barnett said. "I wanted them to act like we knew how to win."

They did from the opening kickoff, never trailing after Steve Schnur's seven-yard touchdown pass to Dave Beazley opened the scoring with 8:45 left in the first quarter.

Sam Valenzisi tied the NU record with his 36th consecutive extra point, then negated a 35-yard field goal by Notre Dame's Kevin Kopka with a 37-yard three-pointer of his own in the second quarter.

Robert Farmer's five-yard touchdown run capped a 10-play, 74-yard Notre Dame drive 2:35 before halftime, but Kopka's extra point try sailed wide right and NU preserved a 10-9 advantage.

NU's third-quarter collapses had become commonplace during the Wildcats' current stretch of 23 consecutive losing seasons, but one didn't materialize this time.

Sophomore tailback Darnell Autry (33 carries, 160 yards) had his longest gain—29 yards—on the second play of NU's first second-half possession, and Schnur connected with another sophomore, D'Wayne Bates, on a 26-yard touchdown pass in the third.

Bates' first collegiate reception provided the rest of the points NU needed to post only its eighth win in the 47 games played against Notre Dame since the first meeting in 1889.

Valenzisi's second extra point followed with the second half 2:58 old. It gave him the school record for consecutive conversions, erasing John Duvic's mark set from 1983-86, and that point would loom big as Notre Dame mounted a comeback.

The Irish closed to 17-15 on Randy Kinder's two-yard plunge with 6:16 left. Quarterback Ron Powlus, dropping back on a pass for a game-tying two-point conversion, tripped over one of his linemen to keep the Wildcats on top.

Notre Dame, losing its first opener since 1986, got one more possession. It consisted of a Powlus incompletion, a two-yard plunge by Kinder, a Powlus desperation pass to Marc Edwards that gained six yards and a plunge by Farmer that was a yard short of a first down.

Defensive linemen Ray Robey, playing his first collegiate game, and Matt Rice stopped Farmer at the Irish 44 with 4:02 to play.

Schnur, giving the ball to Autry on eight of the last nine plays, used up the remaining time before the Wildcats' celebration began.

"It's unbelievable. I'm in shock," said guard Ryan Padgett, no fan of the Irish after a perceived snub by coach Lou Holtz during high school recruitment. "This is the greatest feeling in the world. We established we could play with the big guys."

"I've been gearing up for this one since I was a little kid," Fitzgerald said. "I grew up a big-time Notre Dame fan."

"This win was something we envisioned as a staff four years ago," Barnett said. "We all believed in each other, and it came to fruition. I'm not going to get real giddy about it, but I'm happy for our football family right now."

RICHARD A. CHAPMAN/SUN-TIMES

**Northwestern's Darnell Autry carried the ball 33 times for 160 net yards.**

# GONE IN A SNAP

## NU FALTERS, SPECIAL TEAMS FAIL

*BY LEN ZIEHM*

The euphoria built from the upset of Notre Dame two weeks ago is history now.

Northwestern reverted to its old, bumbling ways in a 30-28 loss to 16-point underdog Miami of Ohio at Dyche Stadium.

The Wildcats (1-1) blew leads of 21-0 and 28-7, to say nothing of their chance to go 2-0 for the first time since 1975, and left with their winless string at Dyche extended to 10 games.

"This is about as low as it gets," said NU coach Gary Barnett, following a 20-yard game-winning field goal by Miami's Chad Seitz with three seconds remaining.

"I feel bad for our students and fans. We created a bandwagon that everybody jumped on. Now they'll slide right off."

The special teams were the heart of the Wildcats the last two seasons. They were to blame for all that went wrong after NU stormed to a three-touchdown advantage.

NU's 21-0 lead looked like it would get bigger just before the first sign of collapse occurred. Fred Wilkerson's clip nullified a 65-yard punt return by Brian Musso.

Instead of having first and goal at Miami's 9-yard line, the Wildcats were stuck back at their own 19. Three plays later Rich Central High School product Dee Osborne—a Miami junior linebacker who is the son of ex-Bear defensive lineman Jim Osborne— blocked Paul Burton's punt. Osborne picked up the loose ball and rambled 10 yards for the touchdown

AL PODGORSKI/SUN-TIMES

## GAME 2
SEPTEMBER 16

MIAMI OF OHIO
**30**

NORTHWESTERN
**28**

**TOP 25**

| | TEAM | RECORD |
|---|---|---|
| 1. | FLORIDA ST. | (3-0) |
| 2. | NEBRASKA | (3-0) |
| 3. | TEXAS A&M | (2-0) |
| 4. | FLORIDA | (3-0) |
| 5. | SOUTHERN CAL. | (2-0) |
| 6. | PENN ST. | (2-0) |
| 7. | COLORADO | (3-0) |
| 8. | OHIO ST. | (2-0) |
| 9. | MICHIGAN | (4-0) |
| 10. | OKLAHOMA | (2-0) |
| 11. | VIRGINIA | (3-1) |
| 12. | OREGON | (2-0) |
| 13. | TEXAS | (1-0) |
| 14. | AUBURN | (2-1) |
| 15. | TENNESSEE | (2-1) |
| 16. | UCLA | (2-1) |
| 17. | MIAMI | (1-1) |
| 18. | LSU | (2-1) |
| 19. | KANSAS ST. | (2-0) |
| 20. | GEORGIA | (2-1) |
| 21. | NOTRE DAME | (2-1) |
| 22. | WASHINGTON | (1-1) |
| 23. | ALABAMA | (2-1) |
| 24. | MARYLAND | (3-0) |
| 25. | ARIZONA | (2-1) |

*"I feel bad for our students and fans. We created a bandwagon that everybody jumped on. Now they'll slide right off."*
—Coach Gary Barnett

that put the Redskins (2-1) on the scoreboard 1:55 before halftime.

Miami could have done even more damage before the intermission, because Osborne tipped a Steve Schnur pass and Jo Juan Armour intercepted and returned to the NU 28 with 46 seconds left.

Two significant things happened before time ran out. Miami's starting quarterback, Neil Dougherty, injured his foot after being knocked out of bounds and Seitz missed a 38-yard field goal on the last play before intermission.

Dougherty's injury led to backup Sam Ricketts taking charge of the Redskin offense, and head coach Randy Walker, a former NU assistant, replaced leading rusher Deland McCullough with Ty King at tailback in the second half. They put Seitz in position for his game-winning kick.

"We didn't want him (Ricketts) to play," Barnett said. "It's difficult to operate against a mobile quarterback. He made things happen."

Ricketts' first pass of the second half wound up in the hands of NU defensive back Rodney Ray, who returned 20 yards for a TD and 28-7 Wildcat lead that lasted into the fourth quarter.

After that it was all Ricketts, thanks to more NU special teams' blunders.

Burton couldn't handle Larry Curry's snap for a 46-yard field goal try by Sam Valenzisi on the second play of the fourth quarter and was tackled for a 17-yard loss. Miami scored with a nine-play 55-yard drive that culminated in Jay Hall's 3-yard TD reception.

The NU gap was cut to 28-21 with an eight-play 68-yard march that Ricketts finished with a 9-yard scoring toss to Jeremy Adkins with 8:16 left in the game. Then came an 80-yard drive that King finished with a 2-yard touchdown with 2:22 remaining.

Miami went for the two-point conversion, but Ricketts' pass sailed over receiver Eric Henderson.

Even with that good fortune, NU couldn't run out the clock. Miami had used its last time out when Burton dropped back to punt from his own 34 with 1:34 remaining.

Another bad snap by Curry led to Burton recovering it at the NU 1 yard line, and the Redskins took over with 43

AL PODGORSKI/SUN-TIMES

**Northwestern players Darnell Autry (24), Gerald Conoway (11) and Chris Hamdorf (4) leave the field in a state of shock after their last-second 30-28 loss to Miami of Ohio, leaving them ranked 29th.**

seconds to play. Seitz' field goal came on the fourth play, after referee Jack Teitz stopped the clock when NU players were slow leaving a pileup.

"It took courage for that guy to make the call," Walker admitted. Barnett had no problems with it, though a no-call would have salvaged a victory for the Wildcats.

# NU SHOOTS DOWN AIR FORCE

## FIRST HOME WIN SINCE 1993

*BY LEN ZIEHM*

Bring back the bandwagon. Northwestern's rolling again.

The Wildcats (2-1) recovered from a devastating loss to Miami of Ohio by pasting Air Force 30-6 in a victory that produced milestones even the season-opening upset of Notre Dame couldn't.

Air Force became the Wildcats' first Dyche Stadium victim since Wake Forest in 1993. They had gone 0-10-1 in home games since then, with one of the losses coming at Soldier Field.

NU also held the Falcons (2-2) without a touchdown. The last opponent to miss the end zone against the Wildcats was Princeton in 1986—100 games ago, when Francis Peay was in his first season as head coach.

When it was over, students swarmed the field, happily ending a week—according to coach Gary Barnett—that started with "traumatized" players and coaches after the Miami loss.

"We went through a grieving session," Barnett said. "But I knew we would bounce out of it. We had to present ourselves as the team that beat Notre Dame, not the team that lost to Miami of Ohio."

The Wildcats did that from the opening kickoff.

They led for good after Sam Valenzisi's 46-yard field goal barely cleared the crossbar with 7:20 left in the first quarter. Valenzisi added two more three-pointers before halftime, marking the fourth time in his NU career that he kicked three in one game.

BRIAN JACKSON/SUN-TIMES

# GAME 3

SEPTEMBER 23

NORTHWESTERN
**30**

AIR FORCE
**6**

# NU DELIVERS A KNOCKOUT PUNCH

## WILDCATS ROLL OVER INDIANA

*BY LEN ZIEHM*

Bring on the Wolverines!

Northwestern tuned up for its upcoming visit to unbeaten Michigan with a 31-7 rout of Indiana at Dyche Stadium.

For two decades, a NU-Michigan game proved a foregone conclusion—but not now. Not after the way the Wildcats (3-1, 1-0) demolished the Hoosiers (2-2, 0-1).

NU hasn't beaten Michigan since 1965, but anything seems possible now.

The Wildcats reached 3-1 for the first time since 1963 with this victory and handled the Hoosiers at Dyche Stadium for the first time since 1984.

The game wasn't even close. The battle of touted sophomore tailbacks was a little closer, but NU won that showdown, too. The Wildcats' Darnell Autry gained 162 yards on 28 carries and scored two touchdowns.

Indiana's Alex Smith gained 136 on 23 attempts, but 61 of the yards came on one carry, and Smith was in Evanston Medical Center when the game ended.

He was carried off the field on a stretcher with 9:32 left. He sustained fractured ribs but fully recovered in the following weeks, allowing him to play in the last 3 games of Indiana's season.

NU led 21-7 when Smith went down, and his absence devastated the Hoosiers immediately.

On the next play—after a lengthy stoppage while Smith was being treated and removed from the field—

**TOP 25**

| | TEAM | RECORD |
|---|---|---|
| 1. | FLORIDA ST. | (4-0) |
| 2. | NEBRASKA | (5-0) |
| 3. | FLORIDA | (4-0) |
| 4. | COLORADO | (5-0) |
| 5. | OHIO ST. | (4-0) |
| 6. | SOUTHERN CAL | (4-0) |
| 7. | MICHIGAN | (5-0) |
| 8. | TEXAS A&M | (2-1) |
| 9. | VIRGINIA | (5-1) |
| 10. | TENNESSEE | (4-1) |
| 11. | AUBURN | (3-1) |
| 12. | PENN ST. | (3-1) |
| 13. | KANSAS ST. | (4-0) |
| 14. | OKLAHOMA | (3-1) |
| 15. | WASHINGTON | (3-1) |
| 16. | ALABAMA | (3-1) |
| 17. | OREGON | (3-1) |
| 18. | ARKANSAS | (4-1) |
| 19. | STANFORD | (3-0-1) |
| 20. | TEXAS | (3-1) |
| 21. | LSU | (3-1-1) |
| 22. | WISCONSIN | (2-1-1) |
| 23. | NOTRE DAME | (3-2) |
| 24. | KANSAS | (4-0) |
| **25.** | **NORTHWESTERN** | **(3-1)** |

*"Our gunners were down there to stop him, but I don't know where the next wave (of defenders) was. There was a humongous gap."*
**—IU Coach Bill Mallory**

NU defensive back Hudhaifa Ismaeli hit Indiana quarterback Chris Dittoe on a pass attempt.

Dittoe fumbled, and defensive end Casey Dailey picked up the loose ball and returned it 43 yards for a touchdown. Sam Valenzisi's third field goal completed the scoring and gave NU coach Gary Barnett a chance to dig deep into his reserves for the first time this season.

Indiana coach Bill Mallory thought the game turned long before Smith's injury. NU led 13-7 when Indiana's Alan Sutkowski boomed a 55-yard punt in the third quarter. Brian Musso, who had a punt return for a touchdown in NU's 20-7 victory at Bloomington last season, fielded the ball inside his 10-yard line and raced 86 yards to the Indiana 6. It was the second-longest punt return in NU history, behind Otto Graham's 93-yarder against Kansas State in 1941.

"That was the turning point right there," Mallory said. "Our gunners were down there to stop him, but I don't know where the next wave (of defenders) was. There was a humongous gap."

Josh Barnes and Fred Wilkerson took care of Indiana's gunners, and Musso had clear sailing until Sutkowski pushed him out of bounds.

Returning a punt from so deep in NU territory was dangerous, but neither Barnett nor Musso thought it was too big a risk to take. "Brian's a great athlete with a big field of vision," Barnett said. "I don't think he knew he was inside the 10."

Autry scored his second touchdown on the play after Musso's return.

Then came Smith's injury, Dailey's fumble return for a TD and Valenzisi's insurance three-pointer. They helped clinch NU's first Big Ten victory at home since a 27-25 victory against Wisconsin in the last game of the 1992 season.

Autry enjoyed his fifth consecutive 100-yard rushing day, which included the last game last season. The last Wildcat with four 100-yard games in one season was Byron Sanders, who topped 100 five times—but not in consecutive games—in 1988.

NU found itself trailing with time on the clock for the first time this season when Autry got untracked in the

PHIL VELASQUEZ/SUN-TIMES

**Darnell Autry had his fourth consecutive 100-yard rushing game this season, with 162 yards and two TDs.**

second quarter. Indiana's 7-3 lead was wiped out by Autry's 42-yard TD run 5:27 before halftime.

"We made some little adjustments," Autry said. "I just kept running, moving and staying patient. I just had to keep pressing until it happened."

# GIANT KILLERS STRIKE AGAIN

## NORTHWESTERN TIPS MICHIGAN

*BY LEN ZIEHM*

First Notre Dame, now…Michigan!

Northwestern's giant-killers struck again, beating the No. 7 Wolverines on their home field for the first time since 1959.

When the 19-13 shocker was history, the No. 25 Wildcats—without a winning season since 1971 and a Big Ten title since 1948—sat alone atop the league standings with a 2-0 record.

"Heck of a way to get to 4-1 (overall)," NU coach Gary Barnett said. "For me, personally, this was a bigger win than Notre Dame because I was tutored in Michigan heritage by Bill McCartney (for whom he worked as an assistant at Colorado before taking the Northwestern job). Plus, this is in the Big Ten."

Northwestern reached 4-1 for the first time since 1963 and started dreaming.

"Six more wins and we go to the Rose Bowl," offensive guard Ryan Padgett said. "The Miami (of Ohio) game was a wake-up call for us (30-28 loss following the win over Notre Dame). You won't see us come down yet."

The win over Michigan, before a dazed 104,642, differed from the other victories. The Wolverines (5-1, 0-1) shut down tailback Darnell Autry, the nation's No. 2 rusher, and the Wildcats won on the strength of their defense.

Autry managed his sixth consecutive 100-yard rushing game, thanks to a 28-yard gain on his last carry,

## GAME 5

OCTOBER 7

NORTHWESTERN
**19**

MICHIGAN
**13**

## TOP 25

| TEAM | RECORD |
| --- | --- |
| 1. FLORIDA ST. | (5-0) |
| 2. NEBRASKA | (5-0) |
| 3. FLORIDA | (5-0) |
| 4. OHIO ST. | (5-0) |
| 5. SOUTHERN CAL | (5-0) |
| 6. TENNESSEE | (5-1) |
| 7. AUBURN | (4-1) |
| 8. KANSAS ST. | (5-0) |
| 9. COLORADO | (5-1) |
| 10. KANSAS | (5-0) |
| 11. MICHIGAN | (5-1) |
| 12. ALABAMA | (4-1) |
| 13. OKLAHOMA | (4-1) |
| **14. NORTHWESTERN** | **(4-1)** |
| 15. OREGON | (4-1) |
| 16. STANFORD | (4-0) |
| 17. NOTRE DAME | (4-2) |
| 18. TEXAS | (4-1) |
| 19. VIRGINIA | (5-2) |
| 20. PENN ST. | (3-2) |
| 21. WISCONSIN | (2-1) |
| 22. TEXAS A&M | (2-2) |
| 23. IOWA | (4-0) |
| 24. WASHINGTON | (3-2) |
| 25. TEXAS TECH | (2-2) |

but Michigan's Tim Biakabutuka was the ball-carrying workhorse. He had a career high 205 yards in 34 tries.

Biakabutuka had 113 yards in the first half to Autry's 28, but Northwestern salvaged a 6-6 deadlock at the break thanks to great defense and two Sam Valenzisi field goals.

Michigan, leading 3-0, had first and goal at the Northwestern 1 early in the second quarter but linebacker Pat Fitzgerald stopped Biakabutuka twice for no gain and Brian Griese's third-down pass fell incomplete.

The Wolverines settled for Remy Hamilton's 21-yard field goal before an unexpected source put life in NU's offense.

Steve Schnur, Northwestern's starting quarterback, was forced out with a stinger in his throwing (right) shoulder. Little-used Chris Hamdorf replaced him and passed to Darren Drexler for 25 yards, Toussaint Waterman for eight and Waterman again for 25. Five plays later Valenzisi concluded the 68-yard, 11-play drive with a 29-yard field goal.

TIMOTHY FITZGERALD PHOTO

**Michigan put up a fight, but Northwestern came out smelling like roses in this 19-13 shocker on Michigan's home turf.**

TIMOTHY FITZGERALD PHOTO

**Michigan fumbles the ball after a punt, and Northwestern's Josh Barnes (17) recovers.**

The Wildcats got the tie on the last play of the half, Valenzisi hitting from 28 yards after Chris Martin recovered Amani Toomer's fumbled punt with 31 seconds remaining at the Michigan 38.

Michigan took the lead again with an 80-yard drive on its first possession of the second half, Griese scrambling three yards for the touchdown.

A 23-yard Biakabutuka touchdown was nullified by a holding call and Hamilton missed a 37-yard field goal try, setting the stage for a Northwestern comeback.

Valenzisi's 32-yard field goal pulled the Wildcats within 13-9 and they took the lead for good after Eric Collier's interception on the second play of the fourth quarter winning the game.

"Northwestern deserves this win," Michigan coach Lloyd Carr said.

*Northwestern reached 4-1 for the first time since 1963 and started dreaming.*

# BRUISING VICTORY

## CATS BLACKEN THE BIG BLUE

*BY JAY MARIOTTI*

The slogan is all wrong. When they asked us to expect victory at Northwestern, what they really meant to say was expect giant-killings, mammoth football moments that move the earth.

You figured the Wildcats could play another century or two and not top the mother of all stun-gun upsets, their fantasia afternoon at Notre Dame.

During this game against Michigan, incredibly, they did. And somehow, this one was even bigger, sweeter and more meaningful, a firmer validation of the program's sudden emergence as a serious national entity. If you doubt that, look as I do at a field covered with sprawled and distraught Michigan players, some crying, others pounding the grass in agony. As they grieve, 15 or 20 prep recruits, who had come to the famous big house hoping to play for the Wolverines someday, are walking right past the fallen bodies, more anxious to catch a glimpse of the celebrating victors from a school they know little about.

"Where's Northwestern?" says one recruit in a blue letter jacket.

"I don't know," says another. "But those boys are good."

Not only are they good, they are becoming the most romantic story of this or any recent college football season. It's as if the sporting gods woke up one morning, in jolly moods all, and decided to reward the long-miserable NU faithful for decades of embarrassment. A program so brutal for so long doesn't often rise up, beat two of the sport's mightiest names in their home stadiums and make an implausible rush into the top 15. But that is where Northwestern will be after the 19-13 eye-blinker sequel, and we only can wonder how much higher they'd be had punt snaps not gone awry and they hadn't lost to Miami of Ohio.

TIMOTHY FITZGERALD PHOTO

**Northwestern kicker Sam Valenzisi kicked four field goals bringing his streak to 11.**

What's most amazing about the story, the ongoing miracle of Evanston, is how the coach and his players have grown to expect such glory.

The shock effect was at a minimum. In the middle of gathering chaos, there was Barnett, showing little emotion as he talked to reporters.

"In my dreams, yeah, I visualized this. I visualized beating Notre Dame and Michigan on the road," he said, not sounding surprised. "I'm sure others never saw it in theirs, but I saw it."

The locker room oozed of the same confidence. This time, the players didn't need to be told by Barnett not to carry him off the field, as he instructed before the Notre Dame game. This time, they knew not to act surprised, which is half the battle in life, as he has told them repeatedly in wiping out the loser's stigma. "I guess they just didn't want to do it," said Barnett, quite pleased. "I'm afraid of heights anyway."

When the Notre Dame victory was followed by the bad loss, players heard the same-old-NU guffaws. But same-old NU would have folded up the season. The new-age Wildcats gathered their senses and broken pieces, routed Air Force and Indiana, then played a smart and savvy game at Michigan. This was bigger than Notre Dame because they came from behind, worked razzle-dazzle like the option pass play from Steve Schnur to D'Wayne Bates to Darren Drexler, made the major defensive stands when necessary.

"We expect to win games, no matter if it's Michigan or whatever," said Ryan Padgett, the offensive guard who helps open holes for running sensation Darnell Autry. "It's a big win, but there are more games to come."

Not entirely. Some players are openly talking about a bowl game, now a probability for only the second time in school history. And why not? NU is 4-1. NU is tied for first in the Big 10. NU has just beaten an opponent it hadn't beaten in 30 years or at Michigan Stadium in 36 years—since Ron Burton, father of current punter Paul, was playing on the team.

This is an outfit with terrific special teams, an offense that works its efficiency around the tank-like Autry and a physical defense.

Think bowl. Dare we say Rose?

**Steve Schnur, NU's starting quarterback, was forced out of the Michigan game with a stinger in his throwing shoulder in the first half.**

53

# NU RALLIES AT THE METRODOME

## CINDERELLA SEASON CONTINUES

*BY JAY MARIOTTI*

It was the perfect place for the bubble to pop, in a domed stadium that looks like a bubble. Yet there were the purple darlings of college football, maintaining the dream, making that New York Times computer hiccup again, landing another romantic blow for the great American underdog.

There was Darnell Autry, dipping right, galloping left, then outracing the cornerback in a half-field sprint to the right pylon. There was D'Wayne Bates, the receiver from former Chicago Bear William Perry's hometown, clutching passes the way Fridge used to clutch Quarter Pounders. There was Steve Schnur, the little quarterback who really ought to buy an insurance policy, shaking off cheap shots to the chops to make big plays. There were the annoying mad dogs of the defense, Casey Dailey and Matt Rice and Pat Fitzgerald, bringing sack relief to every moment of doubt.

The closet skeptics thought Northwestern would blow it. When will they learn the Wildcats are beyond the gag stage, that pain and misery is in the past, that they are 5-1 now and real as a midterm? In a way, they made as meaningful a point in beating a credible Minnesota team, 27-17, as they did in stunning Notre Dame and Michigan. In a way, Northwestern proved it could beat its most difficult traditional opponent of all.

Itself.

For a while there, the scene looked like same old NU. The Cats fell behind 14-3 early, making the errors they didn't make against the national elite: a bad third-down

# GAME 6

OCTOBER 14

NORTHWESTERN
**27**

MINNESOTA
**17**

# NO PLACE LIKE HOME FOR NU

## BADGER BLOWOUT ADDS UP TO BOWL

*BY RICK TELANDER*

Outlined against a blue gray October sky rode the Four Horsemen of the Apocalypse—tuition, SAT scores, bowl dreams and Valenzisi.

Of the four, Northwestern's little place-kicker, Sam Valenzisi, fared the worst.

He blew out his left knee in the midst of Northwestern's 35-0 rout of Wisconsin when he planted his foot too hard on his kickoff at the 26-0 mark, or celebrated his kick being downed at the 3.

His replacement, little Brian Gowins of Birmingham, Ala., reported after the game that Sam V. had told him that he hurt his knee on the kick and that "it was adrenaline" that enabled him to keep running up the field and leap into the air like a giddy ballerina.

Whatever.

Sam V. was in the hospital, and his 11 points on three field goals and two extra points would carry his spirit along with the rest of these 6-1 Wildcats, who look as though they are due for brain tissue sampling to make sure they are actual Northwestern players and not Buckeyes in disguise.

This game was not close. It was almost Florida State-like in its relentless lopsidedness.

Northwestern's first punt—a spiraling beauty, as almost all of senior punter Paul Burton's are—zipped through the arms of Wisconsin returner Aaron Stecker and was recovered by NU tight end Shane Graham at the Badgers' 25 with 12 minutes left in the first quarter.

## TOP 25

| | TEAM | RECORD |
|---|---|---|
| 1. | FLORIDA ST. | (7-0) |
| 2. | NEBRASKA | (7-0) |
| 3. | FLORIDA | (6-0) |
| 4. | OHIO ST. | (7-0) |
| 5. | TENNESSEE | (6-1) |
| 6. | KANSAS | (7-0) |
| 7. | COLORADO | (6-1) |
| 8. | **NORTHWESTERN** | **(6-1)** |
| 9. | MICHIGAN | (6-1) |
| 10. | OREGON | (6-1) |
| 11. | AUBURN | (5-2) |
| 12. | NOTRE DAME | (6-2) |
| 13. | USC | (6-1) |
| 14. | KANSAS ST. | (6-1) |
| 15. | TEXAS | (5-1-1) |
| 16. | PENN ST. | (5-2) |
| 17. | WASHINGTON | (5-2) |
| 18. | ALABAMA | (5-2) |
| 19. | TEXAS A&M | (4-2) |
| 20. | VIRGINIA | (6-3) |
| 21. | SYRACUSE | (6-1) |
| 22. | TEXAS TECH | (4-2) |
| 23. | OKLAHOMA | (4-2-1) |
| 24. | UCLA | (5-2) |
| 25. | IOWA | (5-1) |

Nine plays and two successful fourth-and-ones later, Northwestern quarterback Steve Schnur sneaked in for the touchdown. That was all she wrote.

Wisconsin would fumble four more times—all recovered by NU—and Badgers quarterback Darrell Bevell, perhaps the oldest man with a flattop in Division I football, would throw two interceptions. Northwestern's remarkable running back Darnell Autry would have his 100-yard rushing streak stopped at seven games, but he had a fine day anyway, with 81 yards on 26 carries and one TD rushing and one receiving. Autry would later be credited with 113 yards, continuing his season streak.

This Wisconsin team did not look anything like the bolt out of the blue that won the 1994 Rose Bowl, making one wonder: Do people simply play down to Northwestern's level, or are these Wildcats, like, good?

Here's arguing for the latter.

"We're in a bowl game," is how free safety and team co-captain Bennett matter-of-factly put it. Bennett's book

**Northwestern Wildcats celebrate after their shut out of the Badgers—they are now bowl bound.**

of virtues simply points out the obvious: With six victories and counting, NU has a virtual lock on the Builders Square Alamo Bowl, with a good chance to make the Outback Bowl or the CompUSA Citrus Bowl, or possibly even the thing known as the Rose Bowl, a forbidden Wildcat dish for the past 47 years.

"Right now we're playing with a great deal of chemistry," Northwestern coach Gary Barnett said after the game. And only a handful of his players are tech weenies.

But if the Wildcats are bound by esters and catalysts, they are not merely the product of some rare lab experiment. People can't help thinking of them as underdogs and overachievers, but as Barnett dryly noted postgame, "That didn't look like Cinderella out there to me."

Godzilla, a little bit.

But his point was made. The Wildcats didn't appreciate being two-point underdogs at home to a worse team than they, in front of the first home sellout in a dozen years. It did their newly nasty hearts good to see the rain-geared Badger fans shuffling listlessly toward the exits early in the fourth quarter.

"This was big for us, for getting respect," said Fitzgerald, who finished with a game-high 10 tackles and one forced fumble. "For the last two years, Wisconsin has just flat-out embarrassed us. But I didn't hear a peep out of the Wisconsin fans all day."

When it seemed the Badgers might score a last-second touchdown and spoil NU's first shutout since 1986, the second-string Cats' defense reared up and splattered the ill-fated Stecker for a two-yard loss at the Northwestern 3 as the clock ran out.

Before this season, it was never really clear that NU even had what you could call a second team. It was always a few starters and then brain-surgeons-in-waiting.

But this team works, Barnett said, because the players are good. "Not too many jockeys carry their horses across the finish line," he noted cryptically, before explaining, "You gotta have the horses."

**Northwestern kicker Sam Valenzisi gets attention from the team's medical staff after he injured his knee in the fourth quarter of the 35-0 victory over Wisconsin.**

# CATS COME THROUGH IN CRUNCH TIME

## NU RALLIES IN 2ND HALF

*BY HERB GOULD*

You could have scripted this game before Northwestern and Illinois went out on a blustery day and locked horns.

It wouldn't have taken a vivid imagination to see the eighth-ranked Wildcats finding a way to get it done and the struggling Illini finding a way to lose.

Northwestern won 17-14 behind the running of sophomore Darnell Autry, who carried 41 times for 151 yards, his ninth straight 100-yard game.

And Illinois, after taking a 14-0 second-quarter lead, lost it in agonizingly close fashion.

Blame a defense that got worn down, an offense that sputtered with victory in reach as the clock wound down, and mix in some critical penalties and other assorted miscues.

Illinois (3-4, 1-3 Big Ten), which still has three tough road games left, will have to hope it didn't leave its heart on the windswept Memorial Stadium carpet.

And conference-leading Northwestern (7-1, 5-0) can start planning for a bowl trip.

"I've thought for some time they were an outstanding team," Illinois coach Lou Tepper said. "They don't beat themselves and they have that gun, Autry. He's such a threat, and he opens up other things."

Northwestern has recaptured the Sweet Sioux tomahawk from Illinois and figure to rise to No. 6 in the wake of Kansas' 41-7 loss to Kansas State and Colorado's 44-21 loss to Nebraska.

# CATS TAME THE LIONS

## ROSE BOWL HOPES STILL ALIVE

*BY LEN ZIEHM*

The Northwestern football team already knew it wouldn't be home for the holidays.

But with each passing week, the Wildcats' prospective destination looks better and better.

The sixth-ranked Wildcats (8-1 overall, 6-0 Big Ten) can finish no worse than second in the conference—their highest finish since 1971—after their 21-10 pounding of No. 12 Penn State.

They can qualify for the Rose Bowl for the first time since the 1948 season with two more victories and an Ohio State loss, and they retain an outside shot at inclusion in the bowl alliance. A second-place Big Ten finish likely would put them in the Florida Citrus Bowl.

Chalk up this latest NU upset—the Wildcats' seventh consecutive victory, matching their longest streak since the 1936 Big Ten championship season—to two decisions made before the kickoff at Dyche Stadium.

Northwestern gave away a game ball before the game and decided to break with a coin-toss formula that had been working. And the result couldn't have been better.

Coach Gary Barnett chose this game to honor the memory of Marcel Price, a member of last year's team killed in a shooting accident over the summer in Nashville, Tenn.

A moment of silence was observed in Price's memory before the first home game against Miami of Ohio, but Price's parents attended the Penn State game. They received a football from Barnett at midfield

## GAME 9
### NOVEMBER 4

NORTHWESTERN
**21**

PENN STATE
**10**

## TOP 25

| | TEAM | RECORD |
|---|---|---|
| 1. | NEBRASKA | (9-0) |
| 2. | OHIO ST. | (9-0) |
| 3. | FLORIDA | (8-0) |
| 4. | TENNESSEE | (8-1) |
| 5. | **NORTHWESTERN** | **(8-1)** |
| 6. | FLORIDA ST. | (7-1) |
| 7. | KANSAS ST. | (8-1) |
| 8. | NOTRE DAME | (8-2) |
| 9. | COLORADO | (7-2) |
| 10. | KANSAS | (8-1) |
| 11. | TEXAS | (6-1-1) |
| 12. | USC | (7-1-1) |
| 13. | MICHIGAN | (7-2) |
| 14. | VIRGINIA | (7-3) |
| 15. | ARKANSAS | (7-2) |
| 16. | ALABAMA | (7-2) |
| 17. | OREGON | (7-2) |
| 18. | TEXAS A&M | (5-2) |
| 19. | PENN ST. | (6-3) |
| 20. | AUBURN | (6-3) |
| 21. | VIRGINIA TECH | (7-2) |
| 22. | WASHINGTON | (5-3-1) |
| 23. | SYRACUSE | (6-2) |
| 24. | CLEMSON | (6-3) |
| 25. | SAN DIEGO ST. | (7-2) |

*Coach Gary Barnett chose this game to honor the memory of Marcel Price, a member of last year's team killed in a shooting accident over the summer in Nashville, Tenn.*

moments before kickoff, then were surrounded by their son's former teammates in an emotional tribute.

Barnett said the decision to honor Price was not meant to motivate the Wildcats. "Marcel had a special place on our team," he said. "This was a private thing."

But there was no denying the ceremony created positive emotional feelings. Tri-captain Rob Johnson called it "a kick in the pants."

Barnett thought the coin-toss strategy was the key.

"We won the toss and took the ball," he said. "Normally we'd defer (to get the choice in the second half), but I told the team we'd take the ball and hope for an extra drive.

"It was a psychological thing for both sides. I didn't want their offense on the field, and I wanted ours out there."

Quarterback Steve Schnur guided NU on a 12-play, 73-yard drive that took 6:13 off the clock. Schnur passed 17 yards to D'Wayne Bates and connected with Darren Drexler three times before Darnell Autry (36 carries, 139 yards, three touchdowns) waltzed in from two yards out.

"That first drive was really important," Schnur said. "It's the first time I can remember when (the offense) came out and set the tone for the game."

A 23-yard punt return by Brian Musso to the Penn State 34 got NU rolling again in the second quarter. Autry again scored standing up, this time on a 10-yard run.

Chris Martin's interception put the Wildcats in position to score again, but Brian Gowins was wide on a 44-yard field-goal attempt. Penn State closed the gap with a 73-yard drive that ended with Wally Richardson's five-yard touchdown pass to tight end Keith Olsommer 48 seconds before half-time.

"I was really worried that we were too excited when the game started," Barnett said. "I thought we might play ourselves out early, and I addressed that at half-time."

His fears seemed grounded when the offense had only three scrimmage plays and a punt in the third quarter, but the defense limited the Nittany Lions (6-3, 3-3) to Brett Conway's 24-yard field goal.

Conway missed from 27 yards on the third play of the fourth quarter, infuriating the Nittany Lions and inspiring the Wildcats.

PHIL VELASQUEZ/SUN-TIMES

**NU tackle Justin Chabot opens a hole in the Penn State defense.**

"The kick was good," Conway said. "You could clearly see daylight between the ball and pole."

Schnur put daylight between the Wildcats and Penn State, moving NU downfield with a drive reminiscent of the one that started the game.

The key was a 25-yard gallop on a reverse by wide receiver Dave Beazley on first-and-19 from the NU 41.

Autry finished the nine-play, 80-yard march, running 23 yards to the Penn State one and scoring his third TD on the next play with 11:03 left in the game.

# RUNNING SENSATION SCORES BIG

## RECORD-BREAKING SEASON

*BY RICK TELANDER*

U nderdogs for life, the Northwestern football team is barking hard these days.

The Wilddogs—er, Wildcats—had many chances to lose to Penn State but they ignored them all.

This team seems to expect to win.

How odd. How somebody else. How…troublesome?

At a school that has won 46 football games in 23 years—your basic generation—such assertiveness has left most NU observers baffled, if not a trifle nervous.

How is this being done? Who are these young upstarts? How uncouth must they be?

Well, let it be known that one of them is so couth he can barely acknowledge his own achievements.

That would be the teenage running sensation from Tempe, Ariz., sophomore Darnell Autry, who carried the ball 36 times for 139 yards and three touchdowns in the Cats' 21-10 win over Penn State.

He set records left and right—season touchdowns, 14; season rushing TDs, 13; season scoring, 84 points; season rushing yardage, 1,339 yards; consecutive 100-yard games, 10—but to hear him talk about it all, you'd think maybe he had just been sitting in a basket that was carried up and down the field by porters.

"If it wasn't for everybody else," the 6-1, 210-pound 19-year-old said after the game, "I wouldn't be anybody."

Of his back-breaking 32-carries-per-game average, he said, "I'm happy they have enough faith in me to let me carry it that many times."

**Darnell Autry set records throughout the season with an average 32 carries per game.**

PHIL VELASQUEZ/SUN-TIMES

Which is like Eric Clapton saying he's thrilled his band lets him do so many guitar solos.

Autry's first score came at the end of Northwestern's opening drive. It was a two-yard run designed to go off left tackle, but Autry bounced wide behind a fearsome block by fullback Matt Hartl.

Autry went in standing up that time. His second touchdown run—a 10-yarder in the second quarter—also went to the left and included a block by Hartl.

But on this one Autry sprinted wide, juked, stopped cold, then cut back inside on a dash that could make a Barry Sanders highlight reel.

"They don't have a lot of great athletes," Penn State coach Joe Paterno said. "Except for Autry."

But the theater major would have none of it. Describing that second TD, Autry said, "I was trying to get it inside, but it was congested. I went outside and it was there."

Simple as a clogged nose. And head coach Gary Barnett clearly had the same case of sniffles.

Of his star runner's record-breaking performance Barnett said impassively, "I'm happy for every kid who participated in the game. I'm happy Darnell was part of the team that beat Penn State."

And yet it's obvious the no-man-is-greater-than-any-other-on-this-team credo is behind much of Northwestern's success. It takes real competitors to put their personal baggage aside and submit to the will of the team.

As Autry has.

His third TD was a one-yard burst that followed a spectacular 23-yard hurdling run around right end to the two-foot line.

"You have to have patience, to let the play develop," Autry said of his careful selection of his running lane. "Plus the offensive linemen get (upset) if you run into them from behind. They'll come back to the huddle and say, 'What the hell are you doing?'"

PHIL VELASQUEZ/SUN-TIMES

**"If it wasn't for everybody else,"** the 6-1, 210-pound 19-year-old said after the game, **"I wouldn't be anybody."**

# CATS FRY HAWKEYES

## FIRST WIN AGAINST IOWA IN 22 YEARS

*BY RICK TELANDER*

It seems to this scribe that Northwestern and 9-1 go together about as properly as Art Modell and civic duty.

But there you have it.

The Wildcats are, indeed, 9-1, in first place in the Big Ten, owners of one of the top turnover-takeaway ratios in the country, possessors of we-believe-it-is, and indisputably bowl-bound.

It can't be explained, really, this marvel of change. The Cats thumped Iowa 31-20 on the icy turf at Dyche Stadium, and afterward stellar cornerback Chris Martin said, "No one on this team wants to face losing again."

As if that's all it takes to undo failure.

Martin and his fellow cornerbacks certainly played as though it were that simple.

It was Martin's critical block on Iowa punter Nick Gallery that helped NU receiver Brian Musso return a second-quarter punt for a 60-yard touchdown.

It was Martin's interception of a pass by Iowa quarterback Matt Sherman that stopped a fourth-quarter Iowa drive at the Northwestern 23.

It was Martin's banzai rush that caused Gallery to squib a 15-yard punt just a few plays later.

And it was fellow cornerback Rodney Ray's jarring tackle on Iowa tight end Derek Price with three minutes remaining that forced a fumble that was promptly scooped up by fellow cornerback and nickel specialist Hudhaifa ("Hootie Cat") Ismaeli for Northwestern's final TD.

PHIL VELASQUEZ/SUN-TIMES

# NU GRABS SHARE OF BIG TEN TITLE

## DREAM SEASON FINISHES BIG

*BY LEN ZIEHM*

Northwestern's dream season reached a crescendo.

The Wildcats put away Purdue 23-8 in their last regular-season game to assure themselves a share of the Big Ten championship, their first piece of the league's top prize since 1936.

"This is a huge relief after all the pressure the media—and ourselves—have put us under to see this dream season come to a finish," center and tri-captain Rob Johnson said.

"Not in my wildest dreams did I expect this," quarterback Steve Schnur said. "The championship will take some time to sink in, but nothing can take this away.

"This is something I will look back on my entire life and—for one day—I will be a Michigan fan when they play Ohio State."

The years of frustration ended with NU's first 10-win season, the last nine of which came in succession.

NU's title clincher was produced in the same stadium in which coach Gary Barnett and his staff claimed their first victory in 1992. This one meant much more than that one—a 28-14 mini-upset in the first conference game that year—but it came easier.

The Wildcats took the lead on Chris Martin's 76-yard interception return for a touchdown 7:13 into the contest, struck on another long play—a 72-yard pass from Schnur to D'Wayne Bates in the second quarter—and put the game away with nine points in the first 1:23 of the third.

JON SALL/SUN-TIMES

76

## TOP 25

| | TEAM | RECORD |
|---|---|---|
| 1. | NEBRASKA | (10-0) |
| 2. | OHIO ST. | (11-0) |
| 3. | FLORIDA | (10-0) |
| 4. | **NORTHWESTERN** | **(10-1)** |
| 5. | TENNESSEE | (9-1) |
| 6. | FLORIDA ST. | (9-1) |
| 7. | NOTRE DAME | (9-2) |
| 8. | COLORADO | (9-2) |
| 9. | TEXAS | (8-1-1) |
| 10. | KANSAS ST. | (9-2) |
| 11. | KANSAS | (9-2) |
| 12. | OREGON | (9-2) |
| 13. | VIRGINIA TECH | (9-2) |
| 14. | PENN ST. | (7-3) |
| 15. | TEXAS A&M | (7-2) |
| 16. | AUBURN | (8-3) |
| 17. | USC | (8-2-1) |
| 18. | MICHIGAN | (8-3) |
| 19. | VIRGINIA | (8-4) |
| 20. | WASHINGTON | (7-3-1) |
| 21. | ALABAMA | (8-3) |
| 22. | SYRACUSE | (8-2) |
| 23. | ARKANSAS | (8-3) |
| 24. | CLEMSON | (8-3) |
| 25. | MIAMI | (7-3) |

By then it was 23-0, and the Boilermakers (3-6-1, 1-5-1) managed a consolation touchdown in the fourth after Chris Koeppen blocked a Paul Burton punt. Edwin Watson scored from three yards out two plays later, but the Boilermakers didn't threaten again.

NU planned to throw more against the Boilermakers, but Martin's heroics eliminated the need for that.

In addition to his TD on the interception, Martin blocked a punt by Purdue's Rob Deignan 67 seconds into the second half, then tackled Deignan in the end zone for a safety.

Deignan punted on the next play, and the Wildcats needed only two plays to score again. Tailback Darnell Autry (career-high 226 rushing yards) raced 59 yards to the Purdue's 1. He is the only player in Division I-A to have at least 100 yards rushing in all 11 games this season. Schnur sneaked for the touchdown.

Then it was a countdown to the championship. When it was official, NU fans swarmed the field, players put on white and blue caps that signified their accomplishment

JON SALL/SUN-TIMES

**Darnell Autry pulls away from Purdue's Derrick Winston on a 59-yard run in the third quarter.**

**With a season-ending Big Ten record of 8-0, Northwestern Wildcats donned their hats and celebrated the championship.**

JON SALL/SUN-TIMES

and Big Ten commissioner Jim Delany likened the Wildcats to baseball's 1969 New York Mets while watching the celebrants from the sideline.

"They were the Miracle Mets. These guys were the Cinderella team from the city for the last six weeks," Delany said. "Both came from cities where it's difficult to turn people on, but both did."

Purdue got turned on with one emotional moment. Joliet product Mike Alstott claimed the school's career rushing record on his fifth carry, then toted the ball halfway down the field to present it to his parents.

"That was really special," said Alstott, who played his last game at Ross-Ade Stadium along with 18 other Purdue seniors. "But after that moment, it was a disappointing game."

For Purdue, but certainly not for Northwestern.

"It was a tremendous day," Barnett said. "The way we played may not have been pretty, but these kids gave just an outstanding effort all day long."

*"These guys were the Cinderella team from the city for the last six weeks."*
*—Big Ten Commissioner, Jim Delany*

Michigan's Brian Griese throws another completed pass, leading to the 31-23 victory over Ohio State sending **NU** to the Rose Bowl.

TIMOTHY FITZGERALD PHOTO

# MICHIGAN WIN SENDS NU TO ROSE BOWL

## PURPLE BUBBLE WON'T BURST

*BY JAY MARIOTTI*

No one could make up this stuff. It has to be real. Week after week, we have waited for the big purple bubble to pop open, for some jester to come out and admit his prank, or for some computer geek to say he concocted the scam in cyberspace. Stop waiting, people.

The bubble isn't popping. It is sealed airtight, forevermore.

Northwestern is going to the Rose Bowl. The end zone in Pasadena is going to look like splattered grapes. Charlton Heston is going to show up on a chariot. President Bill Clinton is going to make a phone call. I'm trying to remain cool, trying not to use superlatives, trying to maintain journalistic savvy. It's not possible.

THIS IS THE BEST DAMNED STORY I'VE EVER SEEN!

As a lovely day at Michigan Stadium proved, the feel-good tale of the decade was simply meant to be, just when the sport needed it most. If the Wildcats can sweep through the Big Ten season without a bump, recline in cushioned seats and watch with the rest of us as their miracle comes true, then it was supposed to happen. If Michigan can use ghosts and a potion called Tshimanga Biakabutuka to upset feeble Ohio State, then let's accept it as fate's care package to the laughingstock.

All that's left is to debate whether the Cats rank ahead or behind the Miracle Mets. Too bad a kid with welts on his forehead was trying to smudge it all after the game, trying to pop the big purple bubble when everyone was ready to kneel before it. His name is Trent

TIMOTHY FITZGERALD PHOTO

**The Purple Bubble made its mark at the Michigan and Ohio State game in a crowded stadium filled with a few disbelievers.**

Zenkewicz. He's a hard-ass defensive tackle for Michigan, one of the leathernecks who turned Eddie George into Boy George. So overwhelmed was Zenkewicz about his awesome afternoon, about restoring pride in Michigan football, about making enemy receiver Terry Glenn eat his trash talk and victory guarantee, he went a little daffy.

He started dissing Northwestern. After so many decades of pain, the Wildcats finally break through, only to have some pompous punk in a tie discredit the triumph.

"We should be going to the Rose Bowl, not Northwestern," he said. "I definitely think we're the better team. I wish we could have that game back. I'm glad for them, but we're better."

Let them squabble all winter. Northwestern is off to Pasadena, my friend, the big purple bubble intact. If this is a virtual reality game, someone speak now or forever hold your peace.

*"We should be going to the Rose Bowl, not Northwestern, I definitely think we're the better team. I wish we could have that game back. I'm glad for them, but we're better."*
*—MU's Trent Zenkewicz*

# NU RUNS OUT OF MIRACLES

*BY LEN ZIEHM*

Northwestern's dream season wasn't supposed to end this way.

But it did.

The Wildcats, who were playing in the Rose Bowl for the first time in 47 years, played with the same desire they had in sweeping through the Big Ten this season and, in doing that, gave the mostly purple-clad 100,102 fans in attendance, one of the greatest games in the 82-year history of the game.

But, even that wasn't enough.

At least it wasn't enough to stop University of Southern California's wide receiver Keyshawn Johnson and quarterback Brad Otton. And it wasn't enough to overcome two costly turnovers.

So when they turned out the lights at the Rose Bowl—and on Northwestern's dream season—the scoreboard lights read "USC 41, Northwestern 32."

"It wasn't a fairy tale season," Northwestern University coach Gary Barnett said, "but it was a wonderful season. There was nothing I'd do over. I don't know if losing the Rose Bowl tarnished our season, but it wasn't what it could have been. We're proud of each other. But we didn't win the Rose Bowl, so we have to come back and win it. That's how we'll approach it."

For some, it's already too late.

"I'll walk away from this place saying, 'What if?' for the rest of my life," said Geoff Shein, a fifth-year senior linebacker. "That's a horrible feeling to have."

PHIL VELASQUEZ/SUN-TIMES

**Brian Musso fumbled late in the first half after being hit by safety Sammy Knight in the open field, and freshman USC cornerback Daylon McCutcheon picked up the loose ball and sprinted down the sideline.**

Especially after all the great feelings of this season.

"Of course, the goal is to win the Rose Bowl," senior center Rob Johnson said. "That's what the goal has to be every year. But to change a program the way we did this year is something to behold."

The perfect ending would have been a victory, but USC's potent passing attack and their own costly turnovers proved too much for the Wildcats (10-2) to overcome.

"When you turn the ball over, you're playing against two forces - yourselves and USC," Barnett said. "We turned the ball over twice, and we haven't done that all year…You're not going to win bowl games playing this caliber of football."

The first turnover came late in the first half. The Wildcats were on the attack when quarterback Steve Schnur connected with wide receiver Brian Musso.

*"We're proud of each other. But we didn't win the Rose Bowl, so we have to come back and win it. That's how we'll approach it."*
*—Coach Gary Barnett*

85

***They stunned the Trojans and the crowd with a field goal, covered onside kick and touchdown capping a six-play, 52-yard drive.***

USC's Jesse Davis intercepted a pass and all but ended any hopes of a Wildcats victory in the Rose Bowl.

PHIL VELASQUEZ/SUN-TIMES

Musso, however, fumbled after being hit by safety Sammy Knight in the open field, and freshman cornerback Daylon McCutcheon picked up the loose ball and sprinted down the sideline.

There was some question about whether Musso was down before he fumbled.

"It happened so fast, it's hard to say," Musso said. "The refs called it like they saw it, and I can't change it. I've got to live with it. The game is not going to change."

Actually the game changed a lot in the second half. After closing the first half with a field goal, the Wildcats rode the legs of Darnell Autry and the arm of Schnur, scoring the first nine points of the third quarter to close within 24-19. They stunned the Trojans and the crowd with a field goal, covered onside kick and touchdown capping a six-play, 52-yard drive.

But perhaps the Cats really showed what they were made of after Otton and Johnson hooked up on a 56-yard touchdown pass to give the Trojans a 31-19 lead with just more than six minutes to go in the third quarter.

A one-yard sneak by Schnur and a two-yard run by Autry, who finished with 110 yards to go over the century mark for the 13th consecutive time, put the Wildcats ahead 32-31 with 12:01 to play.

The lead was short-lived, however, as USC came back with a field goal to regain the edge 34-32. That's when the Wildcats committed their second costly turnover.

That occurred when Schnur's pass to fullback Matt Hartl was intercepted by USC's Jesse Davis and all but ended any hopes of a Wildcats victory.

"We feel bad right now, but there is a lot we did this year," said Schnur, who was 23-for-39 for 336 yards. "Looking back on it, none of us dreamed of being in this situation. I wish I could go back and change some things that happened today and we could win the game, but you can't. That's why there's next year."

"We can never duplicate a season like this," Musso said. "Hopefully, we'll never be 3-7-1 again and we'll never be in the doghouse of the Big Ten again. The surprise of this season to a lot of people is kind of what captured the nation.

"In a sense, we can't duplicate it. But getting back to the Rose Bowl…we can duplicate that."

# A NEW TWIST FOR AN OLD CAT

*BY TIM WEIGEL*

For the past few years, former Northwestern football coach John Pont has been living in Japan. But if he had decided to return to Evanston for the New Year, he wouldn't have recognized the place.

NU football has gotten more newspaper space and air time during the 1995 season than during the entire seven years Pont was coach and athletic director for the Wildcats.

When Gary Barnett made the "I'm staying" announcement just days after the Rose Bowl, it was carried live on radio and TV.

Upon the team's return, 8,000 rabid Wildcat fans packed Welsh-Ryan Arena for a raucous, wonderful salute to Northwestern's Big Ten champions. The rally also was carried live on radio and TV, even leading the local late news.

You might expect this kind of coverage in Lincoln, Nebraska, but in a pro sports powerhouse like Chicago, for a football wasteland like Northwestern? You can bet your $25,000 a year tuition, room and board bill on it. Northwestern is now a big-time football program in every way—except the low student test scores.

So how will the Wildcats respond to suddenly becoming top dogs?

Early returns are promising. The players performed well enough to win in an exciting Rose Bowl game. The administration did what was necessary to keep their coach and upgrade dilapidated facilities.

And the fans came through beyond anyone's expectations. More than 60,000 Northwestern loyalists turned Pasadena purple for the New Year in the greatest show of numbers in school history. Once and for all, this shattered the myth embraced by bowl promoters that

TODD ROSENBERG PHOTO

**For the first time in 47 years, Northwestern's name and its proud purple were painted on the Rose Bowl field.**

**For the first time ever, Northwestern was able to keep a successful coach from fleeing to the fabled "greener pastures."**

Northwestern football fans wouldn't "travel well."

We've all been warned many times: "Be careful what you wish for, because you might get it." In just four, glorious months, Wildcat boosters have gotten almost everything they could have wished for in their wildest dreams.

• First win over Notre Dame since 1962.

• First win at Michigan since 1959.

• First victory over Penn State EVER.

• First win over Iowa since 1973.

• First Big Ten championship since 1936.

• First Rose Bowl trip and Top Ten ranking since 1949.

• First time since 1931 three Wildcats won first team All-American honors, and first time since 1970 six Wildcats were first team All Big Ten.

• And perhaps most important of all, for the first time ever, Northwestern has been able to keep a successful coach from fleeing to the fabled "greener pastures." Everyone seems to agree, the pastures have become just as green in Evanston as anywhere else, which is just what every Wildcat fan would have wished would happen.

But the challenges will be totally different from now on. The coaches and players may find it's not as much fun to sustain excellence as it was to achieve it. They may also discover being glorified is an even greater test of character than being ridiculed.

The University has already learned success is a greater test of its systems and facilities. Loyalties were strained last fall in pre-game traffic jams, parking lot nightmares, and ticket lines around Dyche Stadium.

It's all about the pressures connected with winning. Everybody has to work harder in a championship program, because they have to make plans, not excuses. So far, Northwestern seems ready to make that adjustment.

So welcome to the brave NU world of Wildcat football. And while we're talking big-time at Northwestern, how about changing the name, "Dyche" Stadium? A Top Ten program needs a playing field that doesn't seem like it was christened in the name of flood control.

The floodwaters surrounding Northwestern football were turned back last season, once and for all. Gary Barnett, his staff and his players did it, with absolutely no help from Charlton Heston.

# BOWL DEFEAT CAN'T DIM DREAM SEASON

*BY JAY MARIOTTI*

In a wistful, pass-the-Kleenex way, they were more adorable losing the Rose Bowl than they were reaching it. Just as the sky turned a hazy hue of purple, the proudest little team of football players you ever will see showed it wasn't a meteor free falling in the twilight. A sham, this Northwestern rise is not.

We know that now. The day was that special, that inspirational in defeat.

The symbolism was thick, heavy, powerful. A two-decade analogy was being packed into an emotional second half of comeback drama. Down and buried at halftime, the Wildcats sat down with their coach and listened to him preach what he has for four years, that they still could overcome the gloomy outlook and win. Damned if they almost did.

Rather than lose by one of those old scores, 49-10 or 55-13, the Cats put on an entertaining bowl show for the nation and fell 41-32. If not for an interception by quarterback Steve Schnur, who saw Matt Hartl open down the middle but threw it 10 yards over his head into USC's grubby hands, we might be talking about a clever way the Cats could win the national championship. Yeah, the rally turned us all into dreamers again.

"We played well enough to win. We fought well enough to win," said Barnett. "I can't tell you how proud I am of the way these kids battled their hearts out. It's sort of the way Northwestern has been coming back for three years...21 years...24 years."

But as they've been saying all along, they were not telling a fairy tale or dating Cinderella. If NU really was a miracle, that last-minute touchdown pass to D'Wayne

Darnell Autry scored three touchdowns during the 1996 Rose Bowl while marking his 13th consecutive 100-yard running game.

PHIL VELASQUEZ/SUN-TIMES

The Wildcats stayed enthusiastic on the sideline until the bitter end.

PHIL VELASQUEZ/SUN-TIMES

Bates would have counted and not been nullified by a holding call. And that field-goal attempt by Brian Gowins would have curled through the uprights, not bounced off the left upright. And that pass by Schnur would have been on target. And Brian Musso would have been ruled down in the first half instead of fumbling and watching USC's Daylon McCutcheon run the ball back for a crippling touchdown.

"If it was a fairy tale, we would have won," senior Rob Johnson said. "But I'll tell you, I'm proud to say I was a part of this day and this team. I just wish I could get a sixth year of eligibility. I have no problem going out the way we did because we did it with heart."

"I feel real bad about the interception," Schnur said. "But I don't think any of us are going to let this loss overshadow what we've accomplished. You can lose and still be a winner."

And you can win and still be a loser, as Keyshawn Johnson showed in an obnoxious postgame gloat-fest. There was no reason the USC superstar, future gazillionaire and possible first pick in April's NFL draft had to talk trash after his record performance. Let him be the new Deion. NU understands dignity.

Anyone who doubted Barnett's prowess as a coach has been convinced for keeps. Along with his halftime speech and strategic adjustments, he and his staff showed guts. Bursting with energy, the offense buzzed up and down the field, with Schnur repeatedly hitting the dazzling Bates and Darnell Autry chugging those thick legs for pounding gains. After NU opened the half with a field goal, Barnett went for broke and tried an onside kick. Pulling off the perfect give-and-go, Gowins squibbed it, and sophomore Josh Barnes ran beside it in tandem, smothering it after it went the necessary 10 yards. The Cats subsequently drove for another touchdown—and Barnett had revived his program one more time.

The Rose Bowl performance ensures NU will go down as the greatest college football story of this and most any other season. For the short term, the Cats shut up the trumpets and drums of the USC band, which played that annoying processional march the entire first half but quieted down when the Cats came back. Long term, they set the table for another Top 10 season next autumn…and more brains-and-brawn success beyond.

"Does it tarnish the season?" Barnett wondered. "We didn't win the Rose Bowl, so we're gonna have to come back and win it."

*"If it was a fairy tale, we would have won."*
*—Senior Rob Johnson*

TODD ROSENBERG PHOTO

**D'Wayne Bates completes a 30-yard gain after catching a pass from Steve Schnur. The play led to the Wildcats' first touchdown of the game.**

# STRIKE UP THE BAND

*We ingrain in them really, really hard how important it is to support the team, win or lose.*
**—Stephen G. Peterson marching band director**

BY *WYNNE DELACOMA*

For better, for worse, for richer, for poorer, in sickness, in health…The relationship between a college marching band and its football team is a lot like a marriage.

The marriage between Northwestern University's marching band and the Wildcats was deliriously happy when they marched in the 1996 Rose Bowl parade and during the game's half-time festivities.

Not that the NU marching band was ever seriously unhappy with its team. Like a faithful spouse, the marching band and color guard played the fight songs and led the cheers on those dreary fall Saturdays when Dyche Stadium was nearly empty. After games, they serenaded the players in

SUN-TIMES PHOTO

"Rain or shine, win or lose, year in, year out, we're always there," said Stephen G. Peterson, marching band director.

the Wildcats locker room, even when the team was setting records for the longest string of losses in college football.

But the speed of the Wildcats' transition from the worst of teams to the best of teams boggles the minds of even the truest believers.

"In my freshman year, the team was 0-8 in the Big Ten," said Huw Gilbert, a junior from Seattle, who plays in the band's drum line.

"This year they're 8-0. The turnaround has been fantastic."

Persevering through long hauls is a decades-long marching band tradition, one that came in handy when the Wildcats were the worst team in college football.

"[Getting the band fired up] has never been a problem here," said Stephen G. Peterson, marching band director, "because of the extraordinary kind of student you're dealing with. We ingrain in them really, really hard how important it is to support the team, win or lose. We stress how important they are to developing spirit around the school. In a season unlike this one, if they don't do it, it's just not going to happen."

Being there takes a lot of time. During the football season, the band meets for rehearsal and practice four days a week for two- or three-hour sessions.

Few band members begrudge the time, especially this year.

"If you're in the band just to cheer for a winning football team, I don't think you should be in any marching band," said Daaron Dohler, a fifth-year trombonist from Kansas City. "You should be in a marching band because you like to play the music and you like to go out there and do some hard work."

That said, he admits that the thrill of victory is sweeter than the agony of defeat.

"It's been so much more exciting, so much easier to cheer and stay with the games this year," Dohler said. "You're totally focused. The whole country is behind us now."

Band alumni from across the country and beyond contacted Peterson and John P. Paynter, Northwestern's director of bands who played clarinet during the 1949 Rose Bowl festivities, seeking tickets to the Rose Bowl game.

"When I got home [from the Ohio State-Michigan game], there were 13 messages on my answering machine," Peterson said. "One was a call from Switzerland, of all

TODD ROSENBERG PHOTO

**NU's trumpet section set their pitch, motivating the 100,102 fans, many of whom made the trip to Pasadena with the team.**

Northwestern University band member Jack Kinsella and the tuba section set the chant of the Northwestern fight song as the team prepared to take the field for the Rose Bowl.

'One was a call from Switzerland, of all places, a guy offering to come back and play the tuba if we needed him in order to get a ticket.'
—Stephen G. Peterson marching band director

places, a guy offering to come back and play the tuba if we needed him in order to get a ticket."

"I've got one I still have to deal with," said Paynter. "It's an attorney who was in the band the year they went to the Rose Bowl [in 1949], but he elected not to go. He's been faxing me every day. He wants to come and play triangle and sit in the band. He doesn't understand that we don't really have that much room for casual performers."

Paynter summed up the band's reaction to the phenomenal 1995 season.

"There were two things I've observed. With people who have been in the band for a couple of years, there was a lot of mounting excitement because they had not encountered as much winning as we went through this year.

"For the freshmen, there's a kind of naivete. 'What's so special about this? Isn't this what happens on every college campus?' They've never experienced losing here yet. They have to get used to being in a situation where you aren't going to win all the games every year."

Of course. But who ever wants a honeymoon to end?

# SCENES FROM A ROSE-COLORED DAY

*BY RICHARD ROEPER*

If another 47 years go by before Northwestern returns to the Rose Bowl, it'll be 2043 and the 1996 Rose Queen, Keli Hutchins, will be 64.

In the meantime, here are some highlights from the 1996 Rose Bowl, from dawn to dusk:

1. About six hours before kickoff, two children with purple hair were seen milling about the lobby of the Pasadena Hilton. Jenny and Christopher Rocci of Chicago, whose older sister is an NU student, were purple-topped and loving it. "We found purple hair spray in a store," Christopher says, running a hand through his newly dyed locks.

2. Fun fact: Faced with about three hours of float time with no bathroom break, Hutchins partakes of no liquids before the start of the parade. She doesn't even use water when she brushes her teeth.

3. Why do I recognize the voice of the guy doing the play-by-play commentary of the parade for KTLA? Good Lord, it's none other than Bob Eubanks, still sporting that plastic-looking hairdo we all remember so well from his days of hosting "The Newlywed Game." Mercifully, he does not invoke the term "making whoopee" at any point during the parade.

4. Hottest souvenir items that never will be worn again: "Cat in the Hat"-style headgear, striped in purple and white or maroon and gold, depending on where your loyalty lies.

5. Kermit the Frog, perhaps the stupidest choice for grand marshal in the long and illustrious history of the Rose Parade, garnered the biggest reaction from the crowd. Only after Kermit drives by in a vintage automobile do you realize some poor schmo is hunkered down in the back seat of the car for more than two and a half hours, his hand working Kermit's controls.

6. Teenage conversation overheard in the parade bleachers:
   "So where is Northwestern, anyway, like in the

AP/WIDE WORLD PHOTOS

**Willie the Wildcat brought some Evanston flavor to the Rose Parade in Pasadena.**

*When NU makes the tackle on the opening kickoff, it may be the largest cheer ever accorded any play in school history.*

One of the hottest souvenir items at the Rose Bowl was Dr. Seuss "Cat in the Hat"–style headgear, worn by many Northwestern fans.

northwest somewhere?"

"No man, they're in Pennsylvania."

"Oh."

7. Two floats break down in mid-parade and have to be towed the rest of the way. One is Optimist International's "Reach For Your Goals" float; the other, predictably, belongs to the United States Postal Service and is titled, "We Deliver Dreams."

8. Handy tip: If you're ever going to the Rose Bowl, don't drive. Repeat, don't drive. Traffic jams of up to two hours keep many fans from finding their seats until well after kickoff.

9. Really. Walk, take public transportation, helicopter if you have to.

10. Ten minutes before kickoff, it is a buyer's market for tickets. Up and down Rosemont Avenue outside the Rose Bowl, you can find increasingly desperate young men offering to part with their tickets at face value or even at a discount.

11. I get on the press elevator with Charlton Heston. (Turns out he attended Northwestern! Who knew?) As we depart the jam-packed elevator and attempt to elbow our way through the crowd, I make a joke about once again parting the purple sea for the Wildcats during their trip to Universal Studios. He almost smiles.

12. The pregame parking lot scene was dominated by NU tailgate parties. Peter Laimins (Class of '83), an orthopedic surgeon based in San Diego, paints his surfboard Pasadena Purple and joins a host of his Sigma Nu fraternity brothers for one of the biggest and rowdiest tailgate parties. "We've been here since 6:15 [a.m.]," Laimins says. That would be eight hours before kickoff.

13. The Northwestern fight song, as rewritten and sung by a group of alums:

    We can't believe we're here
    We can't believe we're here
    We might win
    We might not
    But...
    We can't believe we're here!

14. With 100,102 people on hand, the majority of them clearly rooting for Northwestern, were on hand. When NU makes the tackle on the opening kickoff, it may be the largest cheer ever accorded any play in school history.

15. Four minutes and 58 seconds later, USC completes an 83-yard drive for its first touchdown. You've never heard such purple quiet.

16. Has there ever been a better one-word cheer in college sports than: "SCHNURRRRRRRRRR!"

AP/WIDE WORLD PHOTOS

**Jay Leno joins the already overcrowded Northwestern bandwagon by welcoming the Wildcats and NU alum Charlton Heston on the "Tonight Show."**

17. NU ties it up in the first quarter. Purple comes back to life.

18. Hey, USC has two No. 10s, quarterback Brad Otton and inside linebacker Errick Herrin. What is this, flag football?

19. The Rose Bowl divided the seating arrangement so that nearly all the NU fans were on one side of the field, with the USC fans on the other side. They could do the ultimate version of, "We've got spirit, yes, we do; we've got spirit, how about you?"

20. With only two minutes gone in the second quarter, USC's Otton is 14-for-21 for nearly 200 yards and a touchdown. Good thing he's only a part-timer.

21. Confirmed it: Darnell's Autry's father, Gene, is not that one.

22. By the way. Heston's wife of 51 years actually graduated from Northwestern.

23. I'm telling you, they're even saying it in the press box: "SCHNURRRRRRRRRRRR!"

*We can't believe we're here*

*We can't believe we're here*

*We might win*

*We might not*

*But...*

*We can't believe we're here!*

Wildcat fans in attendance didn't want the dream to be over.

PHIL VELASQUEZ/SUN-TIMES

*Has there ever been a better one-word cheer in college sports than: "SCHNURRRRRRRR!"*

24. Hey, somebody want to cover that No. 3 for USC?

25. They've actually got big electric fans on the sidelines to cool down the players. This ain't Wildcats weather.

26. Halftime. All the sports reporters who are NU grads pose for a group picture in the press box, leaving behind about six journalists.

27. In the third quarter, I toss myself into a sea of NU fans. Their mood is guardedly optimistic as the Cats kick a field goal to cut the deficit to 24-13.

28. Hey, there's David Schwimmer of "Friends," sitting in the stands like a regular guy, wearing a brand-new NU shirt-and-hat combo and waving a little pompon.

29. Onside kick! Smart. For that call alone, Gary Barnett ought to be able to get another 50 G's out of UCLA.

30. Autry scores, NU's back in the game and I need someone to give me a boost so I can jump back on that bandwagon.

31. The Cats miss the two-point conversion, and for the first time the NU alums in the press box betray their loyalties with a collective groan of disappointment.

32. Keyshawn Johnson, No.3? Anybody got him?

33. This is like a kid's hand-held video game—it's 31-26 and we've got nearly 18 minutes left. If the USC and NU basketball teams played, there wouldn't be this much scoring.

34. A 46-yard field goal for USC, and now we—I mean, the Cats—are down 34-32.

35. "That's a good kick for a college kid," Heston says grimly. It's 5 p.m. PST. Getting more difficult to see the yellow penalty flags that seem to be flying every other play.

36. Steve Schnur throws the fourth-quarter interception that could kill the miracle. It's getting darker all the time.

37. After the game, as the NU players wearily trudge off the field, a helmetless Keyshawn runs through them one more time to do a stupid clown dance in the end zone.

38. Ten hours ago, the NU band was marching in the Rose Parade as the sun was just starting to rise on a day filled with possibility. Now, in the gloaming of a suddenly cool evening, the band members march off the field, many with tears in their eyes.

39. The field is empty. The teams are gone, the bands are finally gone, the fans have filed out. But the final score remains on the scoreboard: USC 41, NU 32. Not only did the Wildcats lose, they didn't beat the spread.

40. A vendor stands outside one of the main exits with a cart full of T-shirts proclaiming, "USC Trojans, 1996 Rose Bowl Champs." The price: $10. I ask him if he printed up shirts for both schools; he says he couldn't afford to do that, so he went with the school that has the winning tradition. Mercenary.

An hour has passed since the final gun sounded. Just about everyone has gone home, but near the main entrance to the Rose Bowl are a few hundred purple-and-white diehards, quietly waiting in the night.

They are the parents, the aunts and uncles, the brothers and sisters, the girlfriends of the 1995 Big Ten champion Northwestern Wildcats.

The sting of this loss will pass. They love these guys.

TODD ROSENBERG PHOTO

**NU sophomore fullback Matt Hartl sits alone on the bench following the Wildcats' 41-32 loss to Southern California.**

# THE 1995 BIG TEN

**FRONT ROW:** Mike Warren, Brian Harpring, Geoff Shein, Danny Sutter, Larry Curry, Rob Johnson, Ryan Padgett, Shane Graham, William Bennett, Chris Martin, Rodney Ray, Sam Valenzisi **SECOND ROW:** Steve Willard, Morgan Campbell, Chris Rooney, Shannon Jones, Brian Rubin, Brian Gowins, Tyrone Gooch, Scott Musso, Dave Beazley, Hasani Steele, Josh Barnes, Shawn Tomes, Adrian Autry, Levelle Brown, Mark Broxterman, Troy Aggeler **THIRD ROW:** Curtis Shaner, Steve Musseau, Mike Golarz, Jeff Genyk, Dave Hansberg, Ron Vanderlinden, Tom Brattan, Vince Okruch, Jerry Brown, Gary Barnett, Craig Johnson, Tim Kish, Matt Limegrover, Gregg Brandon, Ryan Daniels, Greg Meyer, John Wristen, Larry Lilja, Bill Jarvis **FOURTH ROW:** Doug MacLeod, Steve Schnur, Brian Musso, Paul Burton, Kyle Sanders, Eugene Allen, Don Holmes, Matt Stewart, Gerald Conoway, Darnell Autry, Jeff Swenson, Faraji Leary, Hudhaifa Ismaeli, Mike McGrew, Jason Ross

# CHAMPION WILDCATS

**FIFTH ROW:** Shawn Offenbacher, Eric Collier, Fred Wilkerson, Toussaint Waterman, Kevin Buck, Tucker Morrison, Barry Gardner, Mike Nelson Jr., Randy McLain, Tim Scharf, Chris Hamdorf, Matt Hartl, Aaron Burrell, Jason Matiyow **SIXTH ROW:** Matt Fordenwalt, Ray Robey, KeJaun DuBose, Chad Pugh, Graham Gnos, Josh Kolar, James McCaffrey, Bobby Russ, D'Wayne Bates, Matt Henkelmann, Thor Schmidt, Tim Hughes, Marc Lapadula, Larry Guess, Jason Walker **SEVENTH ROW:** Larry Yeager, Stafford Gaston, Mike Giometti, Pat Fitzgerald, Keith Lozowski, Matt Rice, Zach Sidwell, Casey Dailey, John Burden, Mike Davis, Jeff Dyra, Kevin Peterson, Chris Leeder, Nathan Strikwerda **EIGHTH ROW:** Ryan Friedrich, Bryan LaBelle, Justin Chabot, Mark Tomkiel, Gladston Taylor, Paul Janus, Joe Reiff, Tony Dodge, Jason Wendland, Brian Kardos, Joel Stuart, Jon Burns, Darren Drexler, Bo Brownstein, Brian Hemmerle

COURTESY OF NORTHWESTERN

# DARNELL AUTRY

*BY LEN ZIEHM*

**D**arnell Autry could have picked a better time. Getting your first start against No. 2 ranked Penn State, at Happy Valley, is not the ideal way to begin a career.

And Darnell Autry thought he could have picked a better place. Just two months after making the start against Penn State, he decided he was homesick and wanted to return to his home in Tempe, Arizona.

As it turns out, Autry was at the right place at the right time. Gaining a freshman record 171 yards against Penn State and admitting that "he's glad he stayed" at Northwestern only begins to tell the success story that Autry has become.

Autry chose Northwestern because of its academic reputation and the likelihood he would play immediately.

Just two months after the Penn State game, Autry contacted Arizona State coach Bruce Snyder and asked if he could transfer there. He was "homesick."

"He told me that he couldn't talk to me unless coach Barnett released me to talk to other schools, and Barnett didn't release me," Autry said.

Barnett admitted that he took Autry's request "with a bottle of Maalox."

His refusal to release Autry was standard procedure.

"The rules are set up with the knowledge that, until you give a place a full year, it's not fair to the institution," Barnett said. "It's also not fair to the youngster. If you were to allow everybody who wanted to leave at the end of the first semester, you'd have players changing teams constantly.

"The freshman football player has absolutely no life. His only life is practice and classes. His first 90 days of college there's no fun. It takes you three quarters before you're comfortable.

**"You take it game-by-game and try not to think too far ahead. But I'm a huge dreamer."**

"It wouldn't have made a difference who it was. I would have said the same thing."

Whatever Barnett said, Autry didn't leave. "As I kept talking, coach made me realize that what I was going through was normal, and not the end of the world," Autry said. "I got the feeling that he wanted what was best for me."

Autry also received counsel from teammates, parents and friends. "I'm glad I stayed," he said. "They told me if I left, I might be making the biggest mistake of my life."

Autry stayed, but there remains the question of why a player of his potential went to Northwestern in the first place. There were other options - Arizona State, UCLA, Colorado, Syracuse - that might seem more attractive than a school that hasn't had a winning season in more than two decades.

"I'm at Northwestern because I know I can't play football forever," he said. "I want to do other things. I want to learn as much as I can."

Right now that means learning how to be an actor. Northwestern's theater department has produced Charlton Heston, Richard Benjamin and Warren Beatty, among many others.

"I'm pretty excited about acting," Autry said. "I'm learning valuable things in the theater program. I hope I get the right breaks that I can get on TV or in a movie. I have tons of dreams."

And the gridiron has turned into his field of dreams.

Barnett finds himself with a budding star, but not the perfect back yet. Autry still must improve his footwork and blocking and carries the ball in his right arm too much.

"He's had a couple of misreads, but he's an intuitive, instinctive player," said Barnett. "Darnell's going to get better, because he wants to get better."

Darnell Autry carried the ball 355 times for 1,675 yards (4.7 average), finishing fourth in the nation in yards per game.

"Great things are happening," Autry said, "but I want to see what happens at the end. We've got to finish out the season. You take it game-by-game and try not to think too far ahead. But I'm a huge dreamer."

**Darnell Autry, the 6'1, 211-pound sophomore, finished fourth in Heisman Trophy balloting.**

COURTESY OF NORTHWESTERN

# PAT FITZGERALD

*BY LEN ZIEHM*

The precise details of Northwestern's connection with Pat Fitzgerald are blurred, but there's no doubt it came down to a goal-line stand at a high school game in Orland Park, Illinois three years ago.

NU wide receivers coach Gregg Brandon had seen Fitzgerald in an earlier game, then brought defensive coordinator Ron Vanderlinden to see the prospect.

"If you like a player, the position coach comes in and grades him," Vanderlinden said. "When we saw Pat, his team was backed up to its goal line, and Pat made three straight tackles."

Vanderlinden found what he was looking for.

"We needed to get bigger and faster and find guys who could make plays," he said. "Pat was always an instinctual, intuitive player."

Fitzgerald continued making big plays at Northwestern to the point they became commonplace in his junior season. He made 15 tackles in the upset of Notre Dame and became NU's defensive leader.

While piling up the tackles, Fitzgerald also made nine stops for a loss, had three sacks, recovered one fumble and forced another and broke up two passes.

The 6-4, 220-pounder led the Big Ten in tackles all season. But his season ended abruptly when he broke the fibula and tibia in his lower left leg in the 31-20 victory over Iowa with 4:37 left in the third quarter while pursuing Iowa tailback Sedrick Shaw.

A pin and screw were inserted into Fitzgerald's leg, and team physician Howard Sweeney deemed the operation a success.

Fitzgerald's leg was in a cast for six weeks and he was not able to play in the Rose Bowl.

*"Our concept is team defense. We've built from the ground up here. The players bought into the coaches' recruiting spiel. Now we have belief in our coaches and each other."*

Nevertheless, Fitzgerald completed his junior season with 130 tackles (99 solo), topping the Big Ten in 1995. He was named the conference's defensive player of the week three times and shared the honor with the rest of the defense on another occasion.

Fitzgerald led the team by example. He is the consummate team player. The All-American and Defensive Player of the Year did not turn his head.

"It's very flattering," he said, "but I don't deserve the credit. It all goes to my defensive line. They're making my job very easy.

"Our concept is team defense," Fitzgerald said. "We've built from the ground up here. The players bought into the coaches' recruiting spiel. Now we have belief in our coaches and each other."

The unselfish talk is what coach Gary Barnett likes to hear. He squirms when pressed to comment on his individual stars, even if it might help them earn postseason honors.

Fitzgerald has no complaints. He has never thought of football as more than a team sport, anyway.

"I got that first from my parents," he said. "At Sandburg it was the same way."

Parents Patrick and Florence Fitzgerald are the nucleus of a regular family fan contingent at NU games. Patrick holds a supervisor's job at AT&T and Florence operated a home day-care center.

They got Pat started in football when he was 6 years old on a team called the Orland Park Pioneers in Chicago's south suburbs. "I was in second grade, and we'd play with sixth-graders," Fitzgerald said. "You could weigh 60 pounds and play against guys who weighed 90 pounds. If you didn't learn to tackle then, you'd get trucked."

Fitzgerald felt he was getting "trucked" too often as a high school sophomore and considered giving up football, but his parents were against it. "They preached that sports were nothing to quit," Fitzgerald said.

That didn't change with his studies at NU, where Fitzgerald is a junior majoring in organizational studies and attends Mass every morning on game days.

Barnett calls him "a sponge" because he "absorbs everything Ron Vanderlinden can teach him…He's not just a great player. He's a coach on the field."

PHIL VELASQUEZ/SUN-TIMES

**The 6-4, 220-pounder led the Big Ten in tackles all season and was named All-American and Defensive Player of the Year in the nation.**

COURTESY OF NORTHWESTERN

# STEVE SCHNUR

*BY LEN ZIEHM*

Here's just one example of how Steve Schnur's life has changed since he became Northwestern's No. 1 quarterback.

Schnur visited an Italian restaurant near his home in St. Louis during a five-day break between between semester exams and Northwestern's Rose Bowl trip.

"First the owner came over, then he announced that I was there," said Schnur. "It was unbelievable compared to four years ago. A lot of people in St. Louis didn't know Northwestern was in Chicago then. I think they thought I went to Northwest Missouri State in Warrensburg. That wasn't far away."

Schnur noticed a change in attitude much sooner than the restaurant visit. After the Wildcats upset Notre Dame on Sept. 2, his fellow students—after three years—finally recognized him on campus. The only drawback, Schnur admitted, was that it was harder to miss class. Teachers noticed that, too.

Such is the life of a Rose Bowl quarterback who, just a year ago, was part of a campus joke. NU tried a two-quarterback offense last season, with Schnur and Tim Hughes dividing time. It didn't work, and the Daily Northwestern—never a publication to mince words—referred to Schnur and Hughes as "Beavis and Butthead."

Those days are gone. Schnur is now "the man" for NU and Hughes took a redshirt season, allowing Chris Hamdorf what limited playing time remained for mopup duty. Only in the Michigan game, when he completed three passes for 58 yards, did Hamdorf play a significant role in a game. Schnur was at the controls virtually all the time.

The bad days have not been forgotten, however.

"It's been fun reading the preseason magazines and what all the experts said then," said Schnur. "Hopefully, what we read next year will be better than what we read this year."

*"Last year helped me learn through fire. There were tough times. I learned from my mistakes, and I had a lot to learn from."*

Count on it. Schnur came back for a fifth season of eligibility, but the Rose Bowl comes first and serves as a reminder of the two-QB days. Opponent Southern California has been successful with a two-quarterback system, a fact which surprises Schnur.

"There are a lot of subtleties with each guy. It's hard on the individuals, but even harder for the team to get acclimated to one or the other," he said.

"We really preferred not using two last year," said NU offensive coordinator Greg Meyer. "We would rather have one do the job and be the guy. Last year we tried to find that person but both ended up struggling."

Schnur started the last three games of 1994 and ended the year with a .521 completion rate and more interceptions (10) than touchdown passes (4). This season Schnur threw 101 more passes, raised his completion rate to .541 and reversed his TD pass-to-interception ratio, throwing for nine scores while being intercepted five times.

Schnur's passing yardage (1,456) is roughly half that of USC's, which had Brad Otton throwing for 1,532 and Kyle Wachholtz 1,231. In NU's offensive scheme, however, a quarterback's passing arm isn't the most important thing.

"He reads defenses and gets us out of bad plays more than anything," said head coach Gary Barnett, who describes Schnur as a "cerebral" quarterback.

"Last year helped me learn through fire," said Schnur. "There were tough times. I learned from my mistakes, and I had a lot to learn from."

He performed creditably in the spring but still wasn't assured the starting job when Camp Kenosha started, especially after spending the summer nursing a broken foot.

"I went to Kenosha with a new perspective," he said. "Last year I went in thinking it would be my year and wound up down and out. This year I just felt everything would work out, and if it wasn't everything I dreamed of, so be it."

Then the Wildcats beat Notre Dame and the dreams began to materialize.

"The first one I found after that game was my dad (Gary Schnur)," said Schnur. "He takes our games really hard, and he was crazy that day. I was more proud for him than for me."

Northwestern quarterback Steve Schnur had a pass completion rate of .541 in 1995, with passing yardage of 1,456.

COURTESY OF NORTHWESTERN

# SAM VALENZISI

*BY LEN ZIEHM*

**S**am Valenzisi, Northwestern University's 5-7, 156-pound senior kicker from Westlake, Ohio, led the nation in fieldgoal percentage and field goals per game during the 1995 season.

He snapped the Northwestern record in the fifth game of the season against Michigan with a fieldgoal streak of 11 and contributed greatly to the 19-13 upset of Michigan. He kicked four field goals, though one looked more like a knuckleball.

"I topped it," admitted Valenzisi, the first kicker to captain the NU team since Mike Stock in 1959. "I even took a divot, but my technique is good enough that I could get away with it."

It's a good thing because that kick—on the last scrimmage play of the first half—was important personally as well as for the team. It was Valenzisi's second of the game and ninth in a row, enabling him to tie Ira Adler for the most consecutive three-pointers in NU history.

Valenzisi converted from 29 and 28 yards in the first half and 32 and 22 in the second to pass Adler with his streak. He averaged nine points per game during the 1995 season.

"I just kick as far as I can. The other guys on our special team did a great job. They came through big," Valenzisi said.

After this game, his string of 48 consecutive extra points halted with a miss at Minnesota, game 6 of the season.

Valenzisi, a fifth-year senior doing graduate work in journalism, finished fourth in NU history in scoring with 169 points. He trails fellow kickers John Duvic (200, 1983-86) and Ira Adler (188, 1987-90) and tailback Bob Christian (174, 1987-90). Duvic will keep

> **"I just kick as far as I can. The other guys on our special team did a great job. They came through big."**

his field-goal record of 46; Valenzisi will finish in a tie for second with Adler at 39.

His season ended abruptly because of a freak knee injury suffered in the 35-0 romp over Wisconsin at Dyche Stadium.

"Sam had his MRI (magnetic resonance imaging) exam, and he's through for the year," coach Gary Barnett said. The exam showed a torn anterior cruciate ligament as well as cartilage damage in Valenzisi's left knee.

The injury came on a fourth-quarter kickoff after the Wildcats had built a 26-0 lead over Wisconsin. Valenzisi kicked deep to Wisconsin return man Cecil Martin, then headed downfield for coverage. Martin stumbled after making the catch at the Badgers' 3-yard line, and Valenzisi leaped in celebration.

He apparently suffered the injury after landing on the wet turf, but Valenzisi later told teammate Brian Gowins that he may have caught his cleat in the turf while making the kick.

Gowins was appointed to handle field goals and kickoffs for the remainder of the season.

"We recruited Brian with the idea he'd be our kickoff guy and take over (place-kicking) when Sam graduated," Barnett said. "We wanted him to compete with Sam, but Sam won the job."

With the new kicker came a new holder. Backup quarterback Chris Hamdorf holds for Gowins, while punter Paul Burton did it for Valenzisi.

"It's not that one's a better holder than the other," Gowins said. "It's a comfort thing. Sam and I kicked together at practice, from opposite hashmarks, so Paul held for him and Chris for me."

Gowins found Valenzisi a tough act to follow, especially since Valenzisi was a true leader and motivator of the team.

TIMOTHY FITZGERALD PHOTO

**Sam Valenzisi averaged nine points per game during the 1995 season.**

| No. | Position | Class | Name | Height/Weight | Hometown | (High School/Junior College) |
|---|---|---|---|---|---|---|
| 48 | DB | So | ALLEN, EUGENE | 5'10"/193 | INDIANAPOLIS, IN | (LAWRENCE CENT.) |
| 32 | RB | So | AUTRY, ADRIAN | 5'11"/185 | LONG GROVE, IL | (LOYOLA ACADEMY) |
| 24 | RB | So | AUTRY, DARNELL | 6'1"/211 | TEMPE, AZ | (TEMPE) |
| 17 | DB | So | BARNES, JOSH | 5'11"/170 | CLEVELAND, OH | (CASE WESTERN RES.) |
| 5 | WR | So | BATES, D'WAYNE | 6'3"/195 | AIKEN, SC | (SILVER BLUFF) |
| 86 | WR | Sr | BEAZLEY, DAVE | 5'9"/185 | CRYSTAL LAKE, IL | (CENTRAL) |
| 20 | FS | Sr | BENNETT, WILLIAM | 6'1"/190 | TEMPE, AZ | (MARCOS DE NIZA) |
| 34 | RB | Fr | BROWN, LEVELLE | 6'0"/208 | NAPERVILLE, IL | (NORTH) |
| 71 | OL | Fr | BROWNSTEIN, BO | 6'6"/260 | ENGLEWOOD, CO | (KENT DENVER) |
| 12 | QB | Fr | BROXTERMANN, MARK | 5'11"/160 | HOMEWOOD, IL | (MARIAN CATHOLIC) |
| 49 | OLB | Fr | BUCK, KEVIN | 6'3"/205 | MIAMI, FL | (KILLIAN) |
| 80 | WR | So | BURDEN, JOHN | 6'4"/193 | ORLANDO, FL | (BOONE) |
| 81 | DT | So | BURNS, JON | 6'6"/270 | KANKAKEE, IL | (BISHOP MCNAM.) |
| 7 | RB | Fr | BURRELL, AARON | 6'2"/190 | CEDAR RAPIDS, IA | (WASHINGTON) |
| 14 | P | Sr | BURTON, PAUL | 5'11"/185 | FRAMINGHAM, MA | (FRAMINGHAM) |
| 47 | CB | Fr | CAMPBELL, MORGAN | 5'7"/160 | ONTARIO, CANADA | (THE WOODLANDS) |
| 61 | OT | Sr | CHABOT, JUSTIN | 6'6"/285 | OXFORD, OH | (TALAWANDA) |
| 33 | SS | Jr | COLLIER, ERIC | 6'2"/215 | DIXON, IL | (DIXON) |
| 11 | DB | Fr | CONOWAY, GERALD | 6'1"/175 | DETROIT, MI | (DETROIT COUNTRY DAY) |
| 89 | DT | Sr | CURRY, LARRY | 6'4"/273 | GRANITE CITY, IL | (GRANITE CITY) |
| 36 | OLB | Jr | DAILEY, CASEY | 6'4"/242 | LA VERNE, CA | (DAMIEN) |
| 2 | WR | Fr | DAVIS, MIKE | 6'4"/210 | SAN DIEGO, CA | (GROSSMOUNT) |
| 76 | OL | Fr | DODGE, TONY | 6'6"/310 | MCHENRY, IL | (MCHENRY) |
| 83 | TE | Sr | DREXLER, DARREN | 6'6"/260 | KIRKWOOD, MO | (KIRKWOOD) |
| 88 | DT | Jr | DUBOSE, KEJAUN | 6'3"/273 | JENNINGS, MO | (JENNINGS) |
| 65 | DL | Fr | DYRA, JEFF | 6'4"/245 | CHICAGO, IL | (ST. PATRICK) |
| 51 | ILB | Jr | FITZGERALD, PAT | 6'4"/228 | ORLAND PARK. IL | (CARL SANDBURG) |
| 35 | TE | Fr | FORDENWALT, MATT | 6'3"/227 | SEVILLE, OH | (CLOVERLEAF) |
| 99 | DL | Fr | FRIEDRICH, RYAN | 6'8"/270 | STEVENS POINT, WI | (STEVENS POINT) |
| 55 | LB | So | GARDNER, BARRY | 5'11"/232 | HARVEY, IL | (THORNTON) |
| 43 | LB | Fr | GASTON, STAFFORD | 6'3"/230 | OKLAHOMA CITY, OK | (NORTHEAST) |
| 92 | DL | Sr | GIOMETTI, MIKE | 6'3"/234 | LAKE FOREST, IL | (LAKE FOREST) |
| 66 | OL | Sr | GNOS, GRAHAM | 6'3"/276 | BLOOMINGTON, MN | (JEFFERSON) |
| 38 | RB | Fr | GOOCH, TYRONE | 5'11"/175 | BOLINGBROOK, IL | (WAUBONSIE VALLEY) |

| No. | Position | Class | Name | Height/Weight | Hometown | (High School/Junior College) |
|---|---|---|---|---|---|---|
| 13 | PK | So | GOWINS, BRIAN | 5'9"/160 | BIRMINGHAM, AL | (SHADES VALLEY) |
| 84 | TE | SR | GRAHAM, SHANE | 6'6"/260 | THOUSAND OAKS, CA | (THOUSAND OAKS) |
| 1 | WR | JR | GUESS, LARRY | 6'3"/190 | HINSDALE, IL | (SOUTH) |
| 4 | QB | JR | HAMDORF, CHRIS | 6'3"/196 | IOWA CITY, IA | (IOWA CITY) |
| 85 | TE | SR(5) | HARPRING, BRIAN | 6'3"/267 | DUNWOODY, GA | (ATLANTA MARIST) |
| 46 | FB | So | HARTL, MATT | 6'3"/225 | DENVER, CO | (WASHINGTON) |
| 70 | OT | FR | HEMMERLE, BRIAN | 6'7"/270 | LOUISVILLE, KY | (TRINITY) |
| 41 | WR | So | HENKELMANN, MATT | 6'2"/177 | LINTON, ND | (LINTON) |
| 53 | LB | So | HOLMES, DON | 6'0"/240 | SOUTH HOLLAND, IL | (THORNWOOD) |
| 8 | QB | JR | HUGHES, TIM | 6'3"/215 | GRIDLEY, CA | (GRIDLEY/BUTTE COLL.) |
| 3 | DB | JR | ISMAELI, HUDHAIFA | 5'11"/202 | PITTSBURGH, PA | (WESTINGHOUSE) |
| 74 | OL | JR | JANUS, PAUL | 6'5"/278 | EDGERTON, WI | (EDGERTON) |
| 57 | C | SR(5) | JOHNSON, ROB | 6'4"/270 | CHICAGO, IL | (ST. FRANCIS DE SALES) |
| 39 | PK | So | JONES, SHANNON | 5'9"/190 | GRAND RAPIDS, MI | (EAST GRAND RAPIDS) |
| 78 | OT | SR | KARDOS, BRIAN | 6'5"/285 | SPRINGFIELD, IL | (SACRED HEART-GRIFFIN) |
| 40 | LB | FR | KOLAR, JOSH | 6'4"/220 | WILMETTE, IL | (NEW TRIER) |
| 79 | OT | So | LABELLE, BRYAN | 6'6"/304 | KENT, WA | (KENTWOOD) |
| 91 | LB | FR | LAPADULA, MARC | 6'3"/240 | ALLENTOWN, PA | (CENTRAL CATHOLIC) |
| 37 | RB | So | LEARY, FARAJI | 6'1"/205 | BUFFALO GROVE, IL | (STEVENSON) |
| 69 | OL | So | LEEDER, CHRIS | 6'4"/292 | ROCKFORD, MI | (ROCKFORD) |
| 44 | OLB | JR | LOZOWSKI, KEITH | 6'2"/251 | PALATINE, IL | (FREMD) |
| 16 | CB | SR | MARTIN, CHRIS | 5'9"/180 | TAMPA, FL | (JESUIT) |
| 58 | C | FR | MATIYOW, JASON | 6'3"/255 | COUNCIL BLUFFS, IA | (LEWIS CENTRAL) |
| 88 | TE | FR | MCCAFFREY, JAMES | 6'1"/195 | SCHAUMBURG, IL | (SAINT VIATOR) |
| 45 | FB | SR | MCGREW, MIKE | 6'0"/216 | CHICAGO HEIGHTS, IL | (MT. CARMEL) |
| 89 | OLB | FR | MCLAIN, RANDY | 6'3"/200 | ISANTI, MN | (SAINT FRANCIS) |
| 42 | LB | JR | MORRISON, TUCKER | 6'2"/225 | SEATTLE, WA | (ORCHARD PARK) |
| 22 | WR | JR | MUSSO, BRIAN | 6'0"/186 | HINSDALE, IL | (CENTRAL) |
| 23 | RB | FR | MUSSO, SCOTT | 5'11"/195 | HINSDALE, IL | (CENTRAL) |
| 26 | DB | So | NELSON, JR., MIKE | 6'2"/200 | PLANO, TX | (PLANO EAST) |
| 54 | OL | So | OFFENBACHER, SHAWN | 6'1"/270 | CHESTERFIELD, MO | (PARKWAY CENTRAL) |
| 75 | OG | SR | PADGETT, RYAN | 6'3"/285 | BELLEVUE, WA | (NEWPORT) |
| 72 | OG | SR | PETERSON, KEVIN | 6'4"/282 | LOCKPORT, IL | (LOCKPORT) |
| 77 | OG | SR | PUGH, CHAD | 6'3"/279 | OSWEGO, IL | (OSWEGO) |

| No. | Position | Class | Name | Height/Weight | Hometown | (High School/Junior College) |
|---|---|---|---|---|---|---|
| 15 | CB | Sr(5) | RAY, RODNEY | 5'11"/190 | FERGUSON, MO | (FLORRISANT MCCLUER) |
| 94 | DT | Sr | REIFF, JOE | 6'4"/270 | CEDAR RAPIDS, IA | (PRAIRIE) |
| 95 | DT | Jr | RICE, MATT | 6'3"/255 | MIDDLETON, WI | (MIDDLETON) |
| 96 | DT | Jr | ROBEY, RAY | 6'4"/270 | ROCKFORD, IL | (AUBURN) |
| 29 | CB | Sr | ROONEY, CHRIS | 5'8"/181 | MINNEAPOLIS, MN | (BRECK SCHOOL) |
| 59 | LB | So | ROSS, JASON | 6'1"/227 | DAYTON, OH | (MIAMISBURG) |
| 19 | DB | Fr | RUBIN, BRIAN | 5'9"/175 | DETROIT, MI | (DETROIT COUNTRY DAY) |
| 98 | DL | So | RUSS, BOBBY | 6'5"/275 | CALUMET CITY, IL | (THORNTON FRACTIONAL NORTH) |
| 31 | OLB | Fr | SANDERS, KYLE | 6'0"/195 | JACKSON, MI | (JACKSON) |
| 52 | ILB | Jr | SCHARF, TIM | 6'2"/240 | ROCKFORD, IL | (BOYLAN CENTRAL CATHOLIC) |
| 90 | OLB | So | SCHMIDT, THOR | 6'3"/240 | SANTA BARBARA, CA | (BISHOP GARCIA DIEGO) |
| 10 | QB | Sr | SCHNUR, STEVE | 6'1"/190 | ST. LOUIS, MO | (ST. LOUIS UNIVERSITY) |
| 47 | OLB | Sr(5) | SHEIN, GEOFF | 6'2"/224 | GLENCOE, IL | (DEERFIELD) |
| 56 | OLB | Fr | SIDWELL, ZACH | 6'4"/225 | KEARNEY, NE | (KEARNEY SENIOR) |
| 82 | WR | Fr | STEELE, HASANI | 5'11"/170 | GLEN ELLYN, IL | (GLENBARD WEST) |
| 30 | FS | Jr | STEWART, MATT | 5'11"/188 | OMAHA, NE | (MILLARD SOUTH) |
| 63 | OL | Jr | STRIKWERDA, NATHAN | 6'3"/272 | MADISON, WI | (WEST) |
| 97 | TE | So | STUART, JOEL | 6'6"/220 | ELYRIA, OH | (CATHOLIC) |
| 50 | ILB | Sr | SUTTER, DANNY | 6'2"/225 | PEORIA, IL | (RICHWOODS) |
| 25 | WR | So | SWENSON, JEFF | 5'11"/180 | SPENCER, IA | (SPENCER) |
| 97 | DL | Fr | TAYLOR, GLADSTON | 6'5"/230 | MISSOURI CITY, TX | (WILLOWRIDGE) |
| 28 | RB | Fr | TOMES, SHAWN | 5'11"/175 | SAN ANTONIO, TX | (TEXAS MILITARY INST.) |
| 73 | OT | So | TOMKIEL, MARK | 6'6"/304 | CHICAGO, IL | (HUBBARD) |
| 27 | PK | Sr(5) | VALENZISI, SAM | 5'7"/156 | WESTLAKE, OH | (WESTLAKE) |
| 93 | TE | Jr | WALKER, JASON | 6'3"/266 | CINN., OH | (MOUNT HEALTHY) |
| 68 | OLB | Sr(5) | WARREN, MIKE | 6'5"/237 | ANTIOCH, IL | (ANTIOCH) |
| 18 | WR | Jr | WATERMAN, TOUSSAINT | 6'2"/205 | PONTIAC, MI | (DETROIT COUNTRY DAY) |
| 60 | OT | Sr | WENDLAND, JASON | 6'4"/285 | SIMI VALLEY, CA | (ROYAL) |
| 21 | DB | So | WILKERSON, FRED | 6'2"/190 | DETROIT, MI | (CASS TECH) |
| 64 | OL | Fr | YEAGER, LARRY | 6'3"/215 | TROY, MI | (CRANBROOK KINGSWOOD) |